THE ANIMAL BOOK

A Collection of the Fastest, Fiercest,
Toughest, Cleverest, Shyest
— and Most Surprising —
Animals on Earth

STEVE JENKINS

HOUGHTON MIFFLIN BOOKS FOR CHILDREN · HOUGHTON MIFFLIN HARCOURT · BOSTON · NEW YORK

Animals, Art, and Books

The author and his research assistant.

When I was six years old, I was given a copy of *Life* magazine. On the cover was a remarkable illustration of a bird and a tortoise. Inside, I found an article describing Charles Darwin's 1835 voyage to the Galápagos Islands. The illustrations of marine iguanas, giant tortoises, and blue-footed boobies were fascinating. I cut out the pictures, pasted them into a blank journal, and wrote my own captions. The journal is long gone, but I remember it clearly, down to the way the pictures buckled a little from the paste I used to glue them down.

My interest in books and animals didn't begin with that magazine. I had, in fact, already written and illustrated a volume titled *103 Animals*. At the time, I imagined these stapled-together sheets of graph paper to be an in-depth survey of the animal kingdom. My credibility as a nature writer was enhanced by the small menagerie of insects, turtles, lizards, and other local wildlife that shared my bedroom.

When I grew up, I became an illustrator and graphic designer. I founded a business and started a family. Still, I never lost my interest in

blue-footed boobie

above: **alligator**
right: **black bear cub**

Animals!

vervet monkey

nature and science. And thirty-five years after I came across that *Life* magazine, my first book was published. Since then I've illustrated and written — or co-written with Robin Page, my wife and creative partner — more than thirty books about the natural world.

Reading and writing about animals over the years has introduced me to some extraordinary creatures. And I've learned that many familiar animals have extraordinary abilities.

This book brings together more than 300 of these animals — the exotic and the everyday — and describes some of the amazing things they can do.

— Steve Jenkins

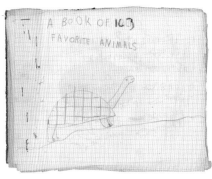

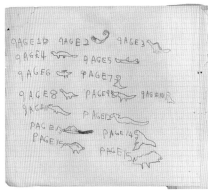

103 Animals, cover and table of contents.

marine iguana and
Sally Lightfoot crab

Contents

yellow hornbill

The blue whale weighs as much as 2,000 adult humans. It is, by far, the largest animal on the planet. The smallest, a microscopic rotifer, is so tiny that more than 150 of them could fit comfortably on the period at the end of this sentence.

Animals are found just about everywhere on earth, and they exhibit an astounding variety. Some are as round as a basketball. Others look like a piece of string. There are animals of every imaginable color — even some whose colors change with their mood or their surroundings. There are blind animals and animals with more than one hundred eyes. There are limbless animals and animals with 750 legs. Some animals have a life span of hundreds of years, while others live for just a few minutes.

All these creatures are doing their best to survive. For most, this means finding food. It means not becoming another animal's meal. And if their kind is to prosper, it means producing offspring.

But what exactly *is* an animal? And why are there so many different kinds of animals?

What is an animal?

Animals vary greatly in size, shape, and behavior, but they all have a few things in common.

Animals eat other living things: plants, other animals, or both.

Animals have sensory organs. They can detect changes in their environment and react to them.

Animals move, at least at some point during their lives.

And animals reproduce — they make more of their own kind.

Animals that eat other animals are carnivores.

Animals that eat plants are herbivores.

Animals that eat both plants and animals are omnivores.

Animals sense and respond to their environment . . .

move . . .

and reproduce.

Millions and millions

Based on the way animals look and behave — skeleton or no skeleton, hair or scales, swimmers or flyers — they are sorted into different groups. A species is the basic group used by biologists to categorize the animal world. Members of the same species usually look alike, act alike, and can mate and produce offspring. So far, almost 1½ million species of animals have been named. Another 17,000 or so are added every year. The total number of living animal species could be 10 million or more.

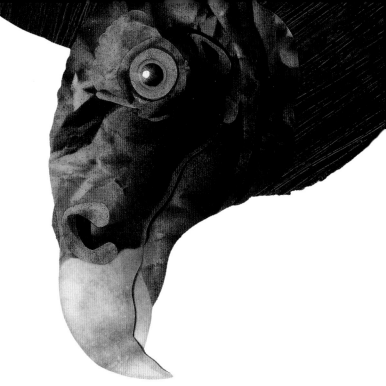

Why so many species?

Deserts, oceans, jungles, grasslands, glaciers: there are countless different habitats on earth. And within each, there are lots of different ways that an animal can survive. In a forest, for example, animals live in the trees, on the forest floor, underground, and in the water. These animals have different diets. Some eat plants or bacteria in the soil. A few eat other animals, alive or dead. Most habitats offer a wide variety of things to eat and places to take shelter, so they can support many different kinds of animals.

These animals — a **turkey vulture,** a **green June beetle,** a **housefly,** a **brown bear,** a **garden snail,** and a **perch** — share a forest home. Each plays a different role in its environment, so the forest can support them along with thousands of other animals.

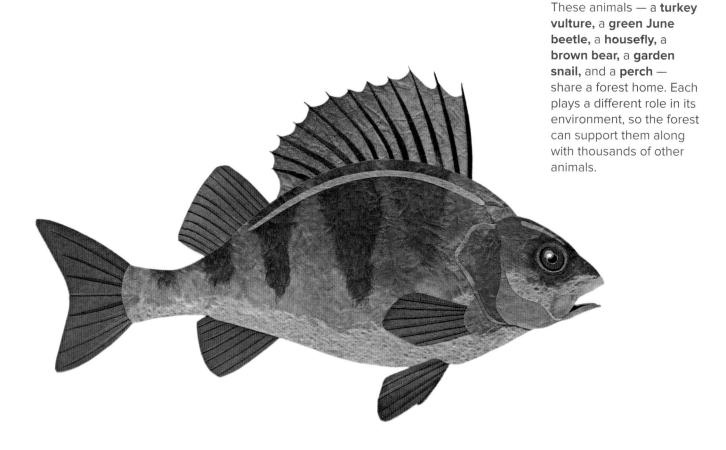

Backbones

Biologists often divide animals into vertebrates — creatures with backbones — and invertebrates — those without backbones or internal skeletons.

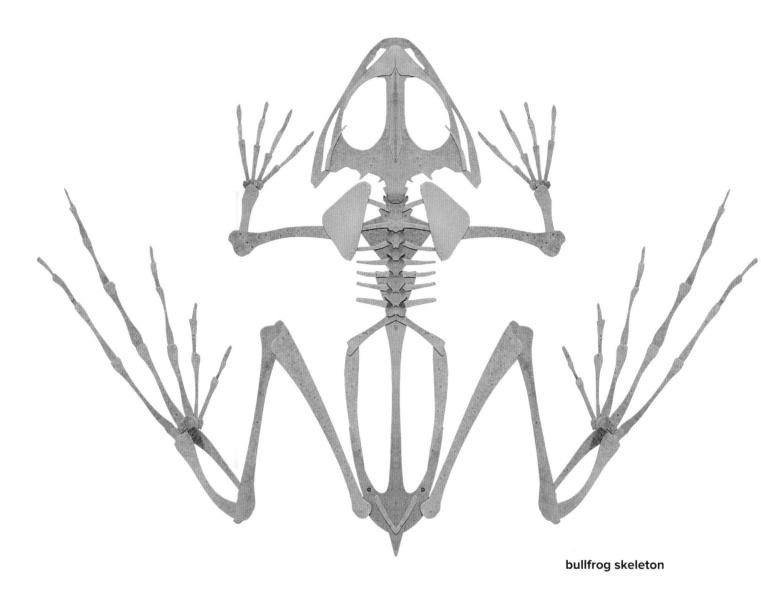

bullfrog skeleton

Fish, amphibians, reptiles, birds, and mammals are vertebrates — they have a backbone and an internal skeleton.

octopus

Most animals — 97 of every 100 known species — are invertebrates. Some, such as worms, jellies, and octopuses, have a soft squishy body. Others, including insects, spiders, and crabs, have a hard outer covering called an exoskeleton.

15

Most animals are insects.

There are a million known species of these six-legged creatures. More than three-quarters of all the animals that have been named are insects.

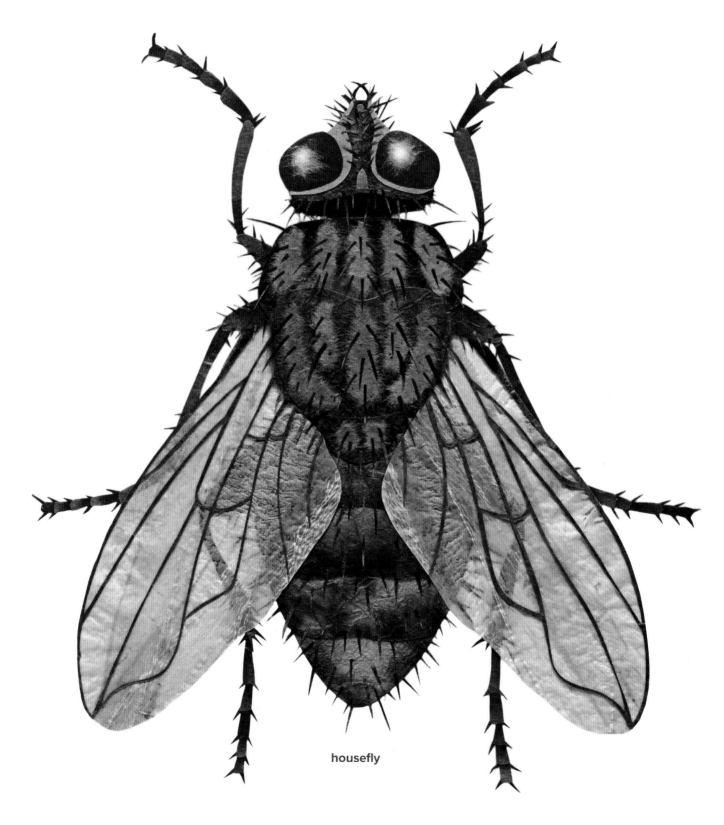

housefly

One group of insects, the beetles, includes more than 350,000 species. In fact, one of every four living things is a beetle.

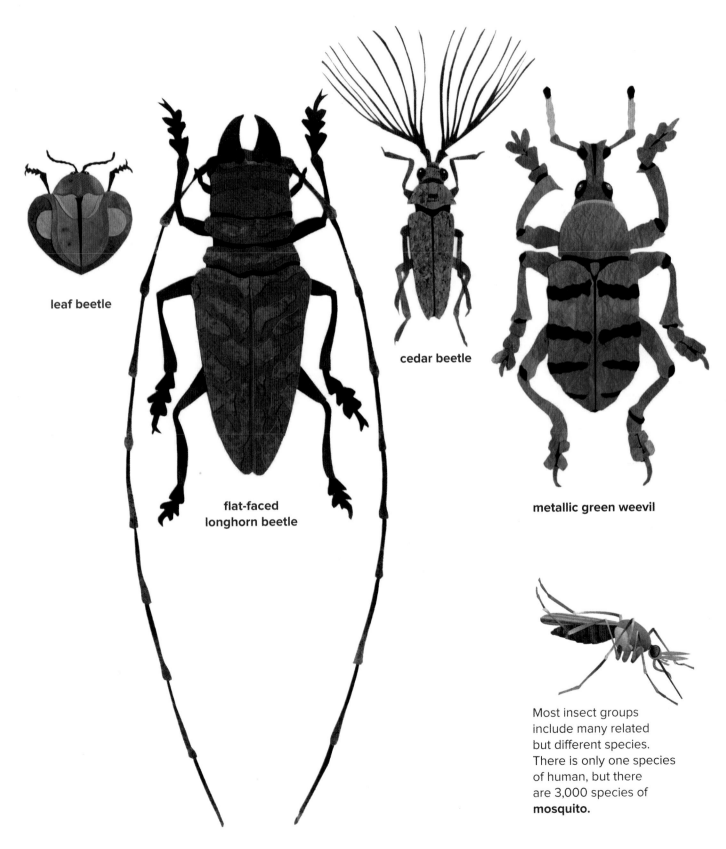

leaf beetle

**flat-faced
longhorn beetle**

cedar beetle

metallic green weevil

Most insect groups include many related but different species. There is only one species of human, but there are 3,000 species of **mosquito.**

More animals are extinct.

The bad news: on average, an animal species becomes extinct after about 10 million years. The good news: modern humans have existed for only about 200,000 years.

For every species alive
today, there are probably
1,000 that have died out,
or gone extinct.

Animal groups

Scientists have developed a system for organizing living things by placing them in groups. All animals are in a group called a kingdom. There are separate kingdoms for plants, bacteria, fungi, and other forms of life.

The animal kingdom is subdivided into smaller groups, as this chart shows.

Vertebrates (animals with a backbone)

fish		Cold-blooded. Live in water and breathe with gills. Most lay eggs, though a few give birth to live young. Includes bony fish, sharks, and rays.
amphibians		Cold-blooded. Born in water. Young breathe with gills. Adults breathe with lungs and can live both in water and on land. Includes frogs, toads, and salamanders.
reptiles		Have scales and are cold-blooded. Breathe with lungs. Most live on land. A few bear live young but most lay eggs. Includes snakes, turtles, lizards, crocodiles, and alligators.
birds		Warm-blooded. They have feathers and wings and lay eggs. Most, but not all, can fly. Birds are the direct descendants of the dinosaurs.
mammals		Warm-blooded. Most have hair. With two exceptions (the platypus and the echidna lay eggs), babies are born alive. Babies feed on their mother's milk.

Invertebrates (animals without a backbone)

sponges		A primitive group of animals. Most live in salt water. Young swim or drift but most adults are attached to the sea floor. They feed by filtering tiny plants and animals from the water. No brain, eyes, mouth, or circulatory system.
coelenterates		Another primitive group of ocean animals. They have mouths and stinging tentacles. Some drift or swim, others do not move once they are grown. Includes jellyfish, corals, and sea anemones.
echinoderms		Live in the ocean. They have external, unjointed skeletons. They can move, slowly. Includes starfish, sea urchins, and sea cucumbers.
worms		Live in water, on land, and as parasites inside other animals. Most are mobile and have soft bodies. Includes flatworms, roundworms, segmented worms (earthworms), velvet worms, and rotifers.
mollusks		Live in water and on land. They have soft bodies and often have hard shells. Some swim, some crawl, and others are anchored in place. Includes snails, slugs, clams and other shellfish, octopuses, and squid.
arthropods		The largest group of animals. They have segmented bodies with a jointed, hard outer skeleton. Includes insects, spiders, centipedes, and crustaceans such as crabs and shrimp.

Numbers of living animal species

These numbers vary from source to source, and new species are constantly being added. But the chart shows the relative numbers of known animal species.

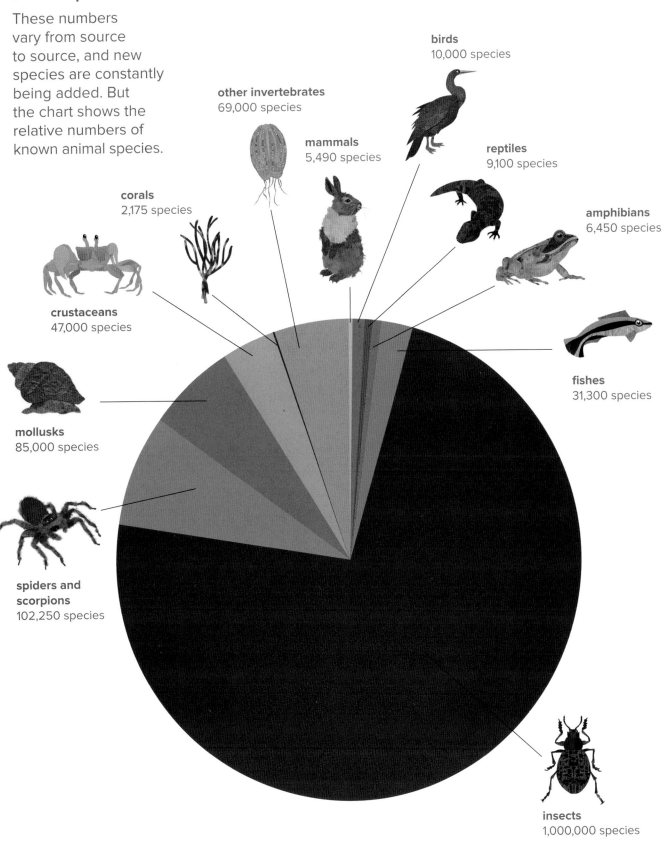

birds
10,000 species

other invertebrates
69,000 species

mammals
5,490 species

reptiles
9,100 species

corals
2,175 species

amphibians
6,450 species

crustaceans
47,000 species

mollusks
85,000 species

fishes
31,300 species

spiders and scorpions
102,250 species

insects
1,000,000 species

Total: 1,367,765 species
Source: World Conservation Union (IUCN), 2011

Family

For an animal species to survive, at least some of its members must reproduce. There are a few creatures — usually simple animals such as sponges — that can make copies of themselves without a mate. Most animals, however, must find a partner of the opposite sex to help them produce the next generation.

I'LL DO IT MYSELF

ATTRACTING A MATE

FIGHTING FOR LOVE

THE MATING DANCE

EGGS

The egg of the **ostrich** is the largest of any living animal.

BORN ALIVE

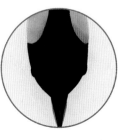

FATHER'S TURN

BRINGING UP BABY

SIBLINGS

I'll do it myself.

There are advantages to bearing offspring without a mate, since locating and courting a partner takes time and energy that could be used to find food or avoid predators. The disadvantage — and it is a serious one — is that parent and child, like identical twins, are exactly the same. There is no variation in their resistance to disease or environmental conditions, so an entire population can be killed off by a virus or a change in the climate.

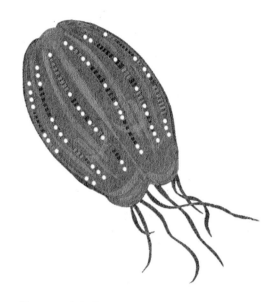

The **comb jelly,** a creature of the deep sea, is both mother and father. It lays eggs, then fertilizes them itself.

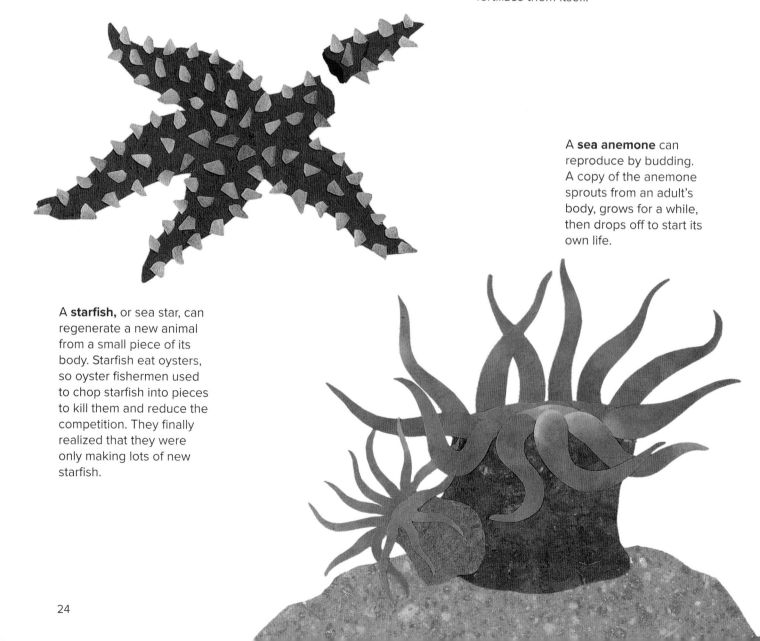

A **sea anemone** can reproduce by budding. A copy of the anemone sprouts from an adult's body, grows for a while, then drops off to start its own life.

A **starfish,** or sea star, can regenerate a new animal from a small piece of its body. Starfish eat oysters, so oyster fishermen used to chop starfish into pieces to kill them and reduce the competition. They finally realized that they were only making lots of new starfish.

There are no male **New Mexico whiptail lizards.** Female whiptails have the ability — unusual among vertebrates — to reproduce without a mate. All the sisters in a whiptail community are identical. They are also identical to their mother, their grandmother, and all their female ancestors.

Attracting a mate

To make babies, most animals must find a mate of the opposite sex. An animal with two parents has qualities of both the mother and the father. This natural variation means that some members of the next generation may be more resistant to disease or better at adapting to new conditions. This is probably the reason that sexual reproduction is so common. But first comes the challenge of finding a partner.

The **deathwatch beetle** taps its head on wood to signal for a mate. At one time, people who heard this ticking sound in the walls of a house believed that someone was about to die. This is the source of the beetle's morbid name.

A male **blue bird of paradise** does an upside-down dance to impress a female. It sways from a branch, waggling its tail feathers and singing softly.

The female **cecropia moth** releases a special chemical called a pheromone. Male moths can detect this chemical — and follow it back to the female — from a great distance.

The male **long-wattled umbrella bird** struts about on the forest floor, hoping to impress a female with its wattle — the long plume of feathers hanging from its chest.

The male **hooded seal** inflates a sac of loose skin that hangs from its left nostril, blowing it up like a red balloon. He shakes the sac back and forth, producing a pinging sound that attracts females and warns off other males.

Wild turkey brothers stay together for life. One of them, usually the largest, is the leader. His brothers help him attract a female turkey by strutting and displaying their tail feathers. They also help him chase away rival males.

Fighting for love

For some male animals, attracting the attention of a female is not enough. Before they earn the right to mate with a female, they must fight off rival males. The loser — who is usually not killed or seriously injured — must look for another female. This behavior helps a species survive because it guarantees that the strongest males are the ones that produce offspring.

Male **Cape stag beetles** use their shovel-like mandibles, or jaws, to flip a rival onto his back. The winner of this contest earns the attention of a female beetle.

Two male **giraffe weevils** wallop each other with their long snouts, much in the way that rival male giraffes strike one another with their long necks.

Elephant seal males wage loud, violent battles to establish space on the beach and earn the right to breed with the females there. The loser, who is often bloodied but rarely seriously hurt, must leave and try to establish a territory of his own somewhere else.

Siamese fighting fish battle fiercely for the right to mate. In Thailand, where these fish are bred for their aggressiveness, people wager huge sums of money on the outcome of a fight.

King cobra males wrestle one another to decide who gets to mate with a nearby female. The snake whose head is first pushed to the ground loses the contest and slithers away.

In a tree high above the forest floor, male **stag beetles** lock horns. The loser is tossed from his perch and misses his opportunity to mate.

The mating dance

Once they've found each other, males
and females of many animal species
go through a complex mating ritual.
Sometimes this creates a bond that will
help when it's time for the parents to
raise a family. In other cases, it's a chance
for the animals to judge each other's
health and fitness before mating.

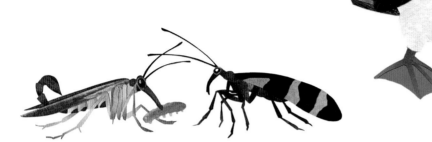

A male **scorpion fly**
presents a gift — usually
a worm or insect — to a
female. If she accepts it,
they will become mates.

The male **blue-footed
booby** performs a dance
for a female, lifting his
feet high and displaying
them to her. She seems
to prefer males with the
bluest feet.

Before they mate, a pair
of **arctic hares** leap into
the air and tumble about,
sometimes somersaulting
over each other.

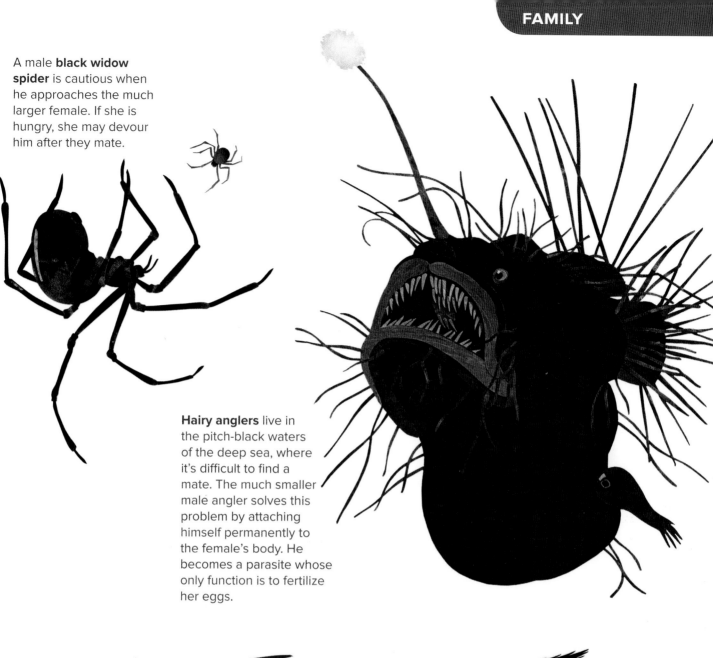

A male **black widow spider** is cautious when he approaches the much larger female. If she is hungry, she may devour him after they mate.

Hairy anglers live in the pitch-black waters of the deep sea, where it's difficult to find a mate. The much smaller male angler solves this problem by attaching himself permanently to the female's body. He becomes a parasite whose only function is to fertilize her eggs.

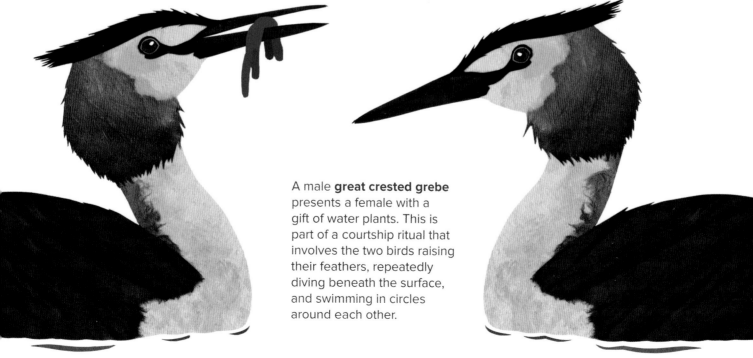

A male **great crested grebe** presents a female with a gift of water plants. This is part of a courtship ritual that involves the two birds raising their feathers, repeatedly diving beneath the surface, and swimming in circles around each other.

Eggs

Although some animals can split off part of their body and make a copy of themselves, most reproduce by laying eggs or giving birth to live babies. Some egg-laying animals produce hundreds, thousands, or millions of eggs. These animals usually leave their eggs and young to fend for themselves — there are so many offspring that a handful will probably survive on their own. Other egg-layers produce just a few eggs — perhaps only one. These animals often protect their eggs and watch over their young after they hatch.

The **echidna** and the platypus are the only egg-laying mammals. An echidna mother lays a single egg, which she carries in a pouch on her belly. After it hatches, the baby, which is called a puggle, will remain in the pouch for six to eight weeks.

The **ocean sunfish** lays as many as 300 million eggs at a time.

Employing spider-web silk or plant fibers as thread, the **tailorbird** uses her beak as a needle and stitches the sides of a leaf together, creating a nest that will protect her eggs.

A female **burying beetle** locates a dead animal, covers its body with dirt, and lays her eggs nearby. The carcass will provide food for the beetle larvae after they hatch.

The **ichneumon wasp** (*ik-**noo**-muhn*) injects its eggs into the body of a live caterpillar. When the eggs hatch, the larvae consume the caterpillar from the inside out before emerging.

The **white tern** lays a single egg, often balancing it on a tree branch. This saves the trouble of building a nest, but the technique is risky — the egg may fall and break. The mother bird will quickly lay another egg if something happens to the first one.

A female **Polynesian megapode** lays her eggs near the rim of an active volcano. She doesn't have to sit on the nest to keep her eggs warm — volcanic ashes will incubate the eggs until they hatch.

Displaying behavior that is unusual for an insect, an **earwig** mother cleans and protects her eggs. She will also take care of her babies after they are born.

33

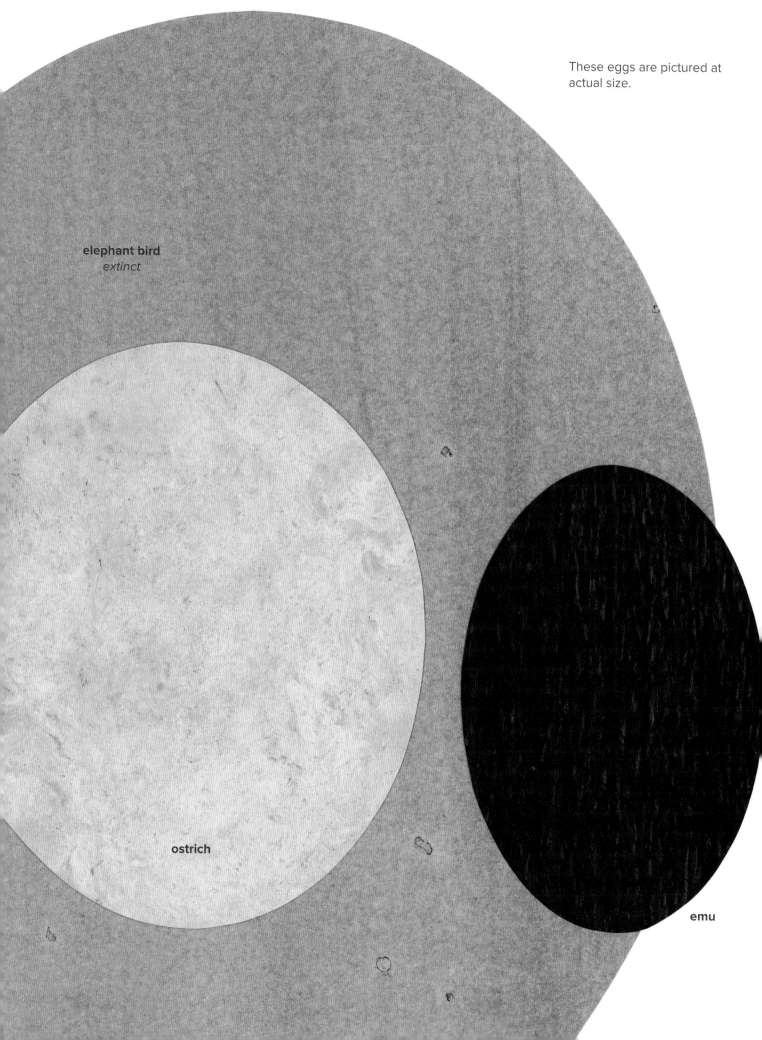

These eggs are pictured at actual size.

elephant bird
extinct

ostrich

emu

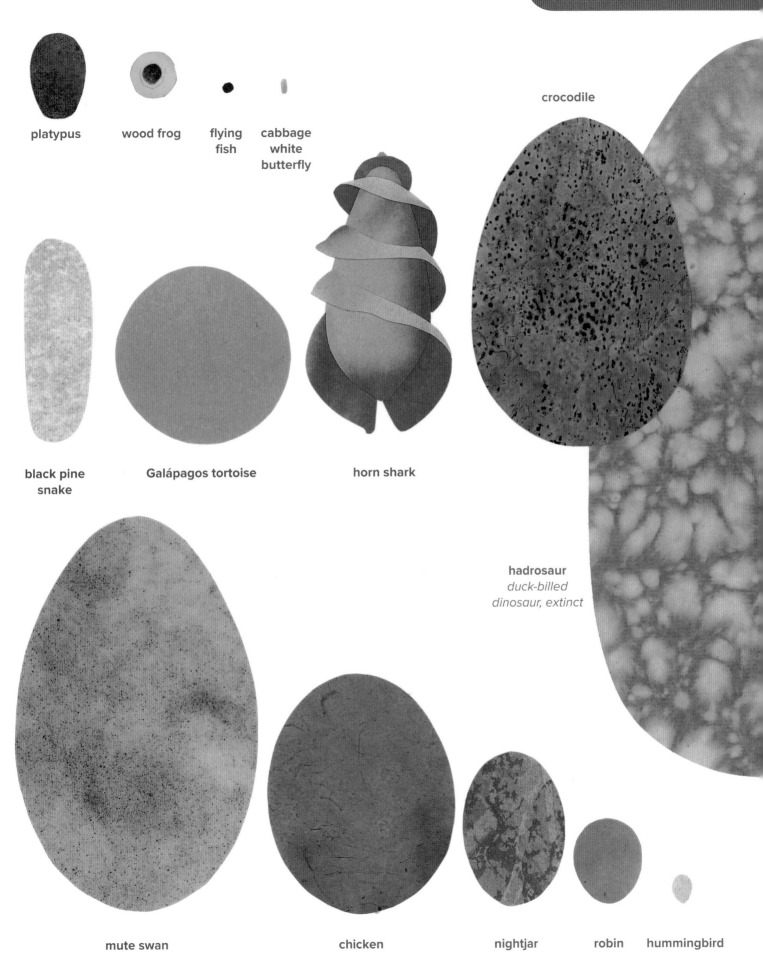

platypus

wood frog

flying fish

cabbage white butterfly

crocodile

black pine snake

Galápagos tortoise

horn shark

hadrosaur
duck-billed dinosaur, extinct

mute swan

chicken

nightjar

robin

hummingbird

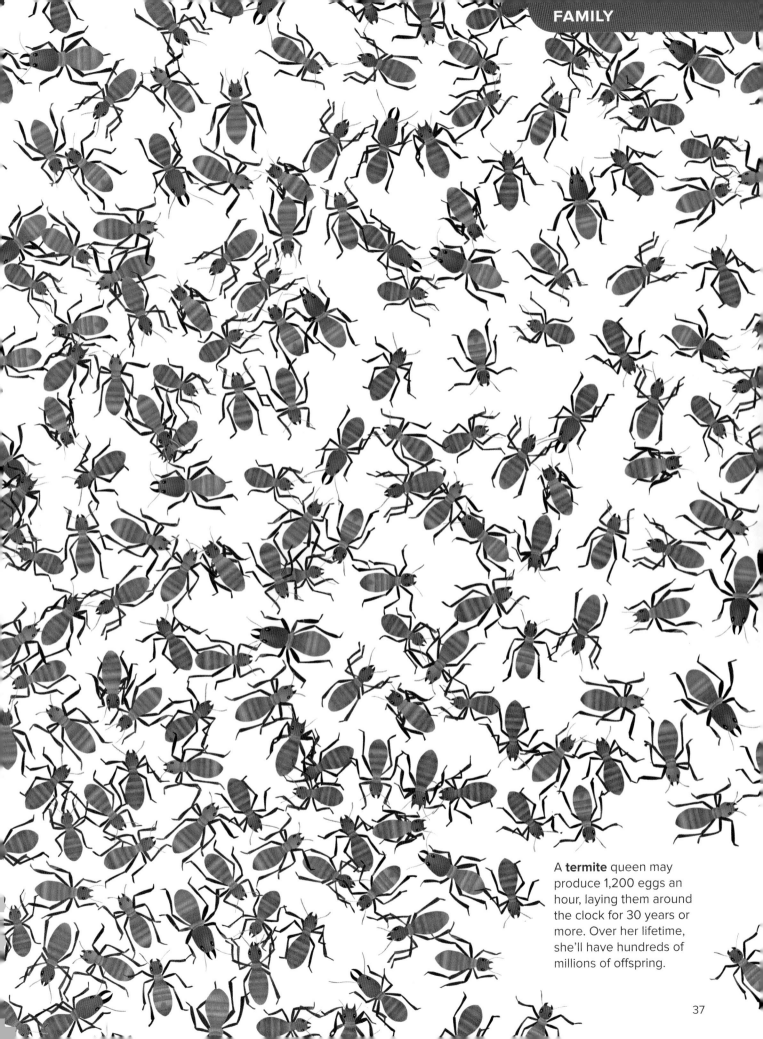

A **termite** queen may produce 1,200 eggs an hour, laying them around the clock for 30 years or more. Over her lifetime, she'll have hundreds of millions of offspring.

Born alive

Almost all mammals bear their young alive. A few amphibians, fish, and reptiles also give birth to live babies. But these newborn animals begin their lives in very different ways.

A **giraffe** mother gives birth standing up, and her newborn calf falls five feet (1½ meters) or more to the ground, landing in a heap. But the baby isn't hurt, and it will be up and walking within minutes.

Baby **Surinam toads** begin their lives in a most unusual way. They are born alive, emerging from pockets in their mother's back. But they actually start out as eggs. As soon as the mother lays them, the father presses them into the skin of her back. The eggs sink in, forming pits. Tadpoles hatch from the eggs, and in a few months, after they've become little toads, they push their way out.

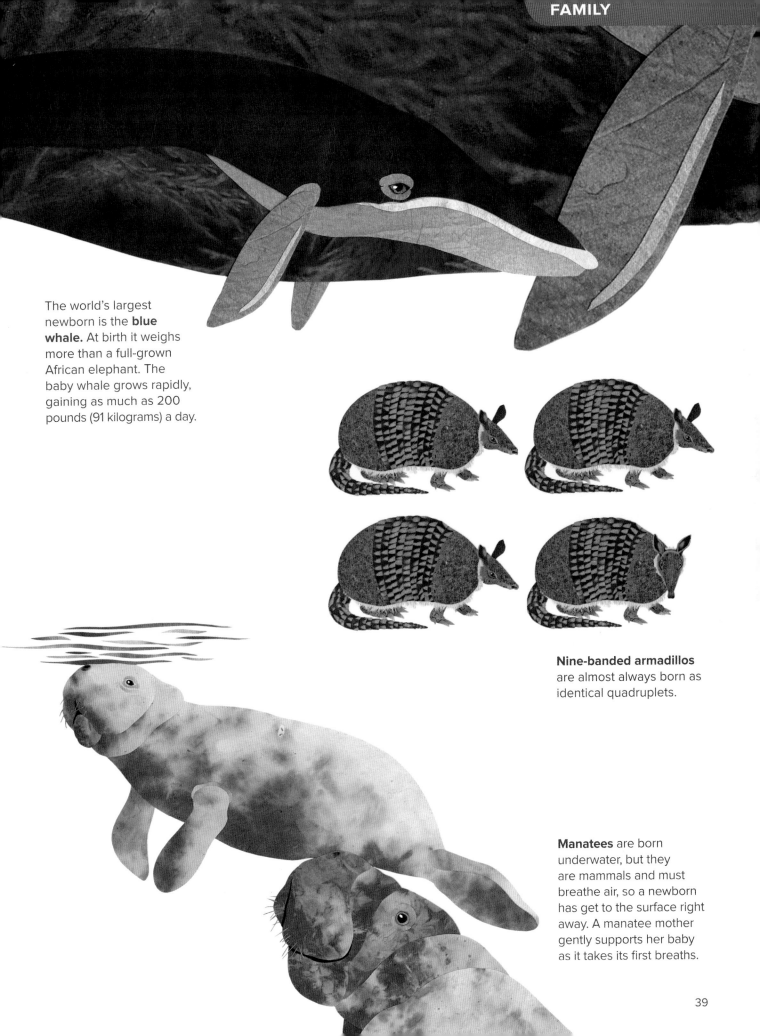

The world's largest newborn is the **blue whale.** At birth it weighs more than a full-grown African elephant. The baby whale grows rapidly, gaining as much as 200 pounds (91 kilograms) a day.

Nine-banded armadillos are almost always born as identical quadruplets.

Manatees are born underwater, but they are mammals and must breathe air, so a newborn has get to the surface right away. A manatee mother gently supports her baby as it takes its first breaths.

Father's turn

Laying eggs, having babies, raising children — for most animals, these things are a mother's job. But some fathers help out, and a few take on most of the child-bearing and child-raising jobs.

A female **seahorse** places her eggs in a pouch on her mate's stomach. Most seahorse fathers carry 100 eggs or more, keeping them safe until they hatch.

When **Darwin's frog** eggs hatch, the father scoops up the tadpoles and puts them in a special pouch in his throat. There they remain until they've turned into frogs. Then the father opens his mouth and the little frogs — as many as twenty of them — hop out.

After a female **blackchin tilapia** lays her eggs, the father picks them up and carries them in his mouth. A week or so later they hatch. He will carry the baby fish — some 50 of them — in his mouth for another week or so, keeping them safe.

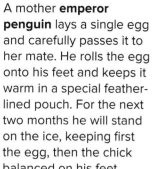

A mother **emperor penguin** lays a single egg and carefully passes it to her mate. He rolls the egg onto his feet and keeps it warm in a special feather-lined pouch. For the next two months he will stand on the ice, keeping first the egg, then the chick balanced on his feet.

A mother **giant water bug** glues her clutch of eggs to her mate's back. He carries them and strokes them with his back legs to keep them clean. The eggs hatch after a week or two.

41

Bringing up baby

When an animal is born, it may be completely on its own or, like us, it may have parents that feed and protect it. Animals that give birth to dozens of babies often abandon the youngsters to fend for themselves. Parents with just a few babies have more invested in each of their offspring, and they often take an active role in their children's care.

A family of **shrews** makes its way across the forest floor at night. A baby shrew could easily get lost, so the group forms a line. The mother leads and each little shrew holds on to the brother or sister in front with its teeth.

Mother and father **parent bugs** guard and clean their babies — something few insects do.

A mother **pelican**, just back from a fishing expedition, regurgitates food for her chick. Many birds feed their young this way.

When danger threatens, baby **alligators** clamber into a nearby parent's mouth, where they are carefully protected.

A young **sifaka** is carried on its mother's back as she lopes from tree to tree. The baby wouldn't be able to keep up on its own.

A father **gorilla** builds a nest of leaves and grass and snuggles with his baby for the night.

Though it can walk, a baby **giant anteater** spends much of its first year clinging to its mother's back. This keeps it safe from predators. Giant anteaters have only one baby at a time, and they are very protective of their young.

Siblings

For many young animals, growing up with brothers and sisters is a good thing. Some youngsters play games that teach hunting or survival skills. In other animal families, older siblings babysit their younger brothers and sisters, keeping them safe. But not all animal siblings are so lucky.

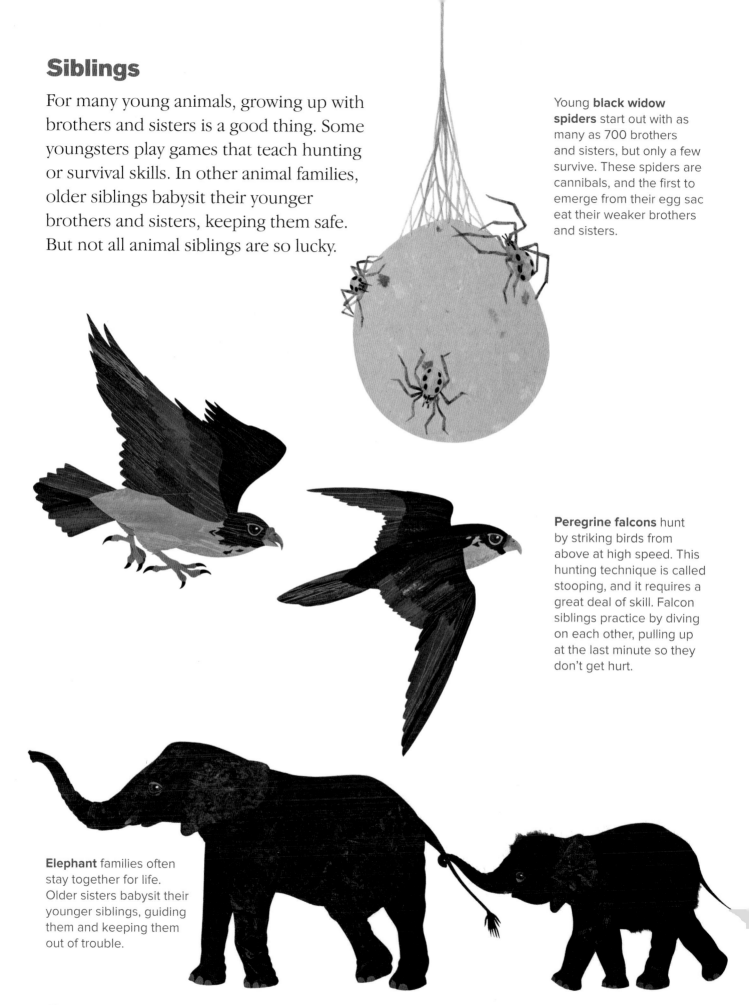

Young **black widow spiders** start out with as many as 700 brothers and sisters, but only a few survive. These spiders are cannibals, and the first to emerge from their egg sac eat their weaker brothers and sisters.

Peregrine falcons hunt by striking birds from above at high speed. This hunting technique is called stooping, and it requires a great deal of skill. Falcon siblings practice by diving on each other, pulling up at the last minute so they don't get hurt.

Elephant families often stay together for life. Older sisters babysit their younger siblings, guiding them and keeping them out of trouble.

Like young lions and tigers, **kittens** play stalking, pouncing, and grabbing games — practice for real hunting when they are grown up.

These two **myna bird** chicks will be raised alongside their much larger stepbrother — an **Asian koel** (*koh-uhl*) chick, whose mother snuck her egg into the myna bird's nest. The mother myna doesn't seem to realize that this oversize baby is not her own, and she will take care of it.

How many days does it take for an egg to hatch?

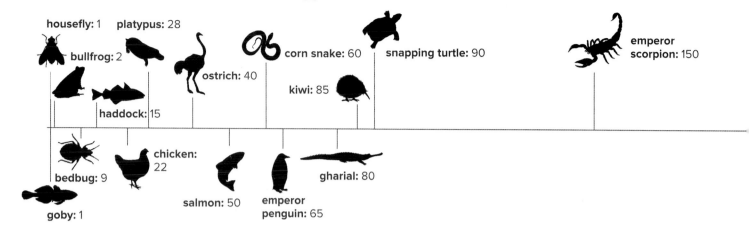

housefly: 1 platypus: 28

bullfrog: 2

haddock: 15

ostrich: 40

corn snake: 60

kiwi: 85

snapping turtle: 90

emperor scorpion: 150

bedbug: 9

chicken: 22

goby: 1

salmon: 50

emperor penguin: 65

gharial: 80

Mammal gestation periods (days)

Gestation is the period between conception — when a male and female mate — and birth. Usually the larger the animal, the longer the gestation period.

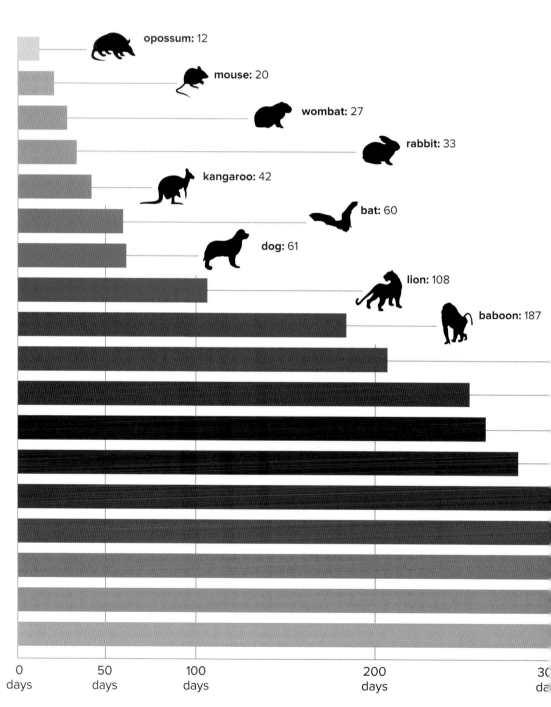

opossum: 12

mouse: 20

wombat: 27

rabbit: 33

kangaroo: 42

bat: 60

dog: 61

lion: 108

baboon: 187

0 days   50 days   100 days   200 days   30 da

gravid chameleon: 215

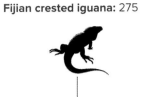
Fijian crested iguana: 275

brine shrimp: up to 15 years

cicada: 240

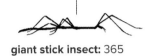
giant stick insect: 365

Number of eggs laid at one time

Philippine eagle (every 2–3 years)	1	**termite queen***	2,000
kiwi	1	**bullfrog**	20,000
chicken	1	**cane toad**	50,000
ostrich	10	**octopus**	150,000
gray partridge	18	**cod**	6,000,000
snapping turtle	30	**ocean sunfish**	300,000,000
leatherback sea turtle	80		
Indian python	100		
mosquito	300		

* In one day. Termite queens can lay around the clock for more than 30 years.

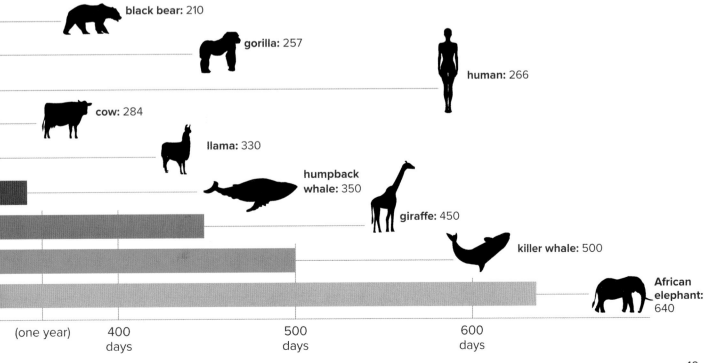

black bear: 210

gorilla: 257

human: 266

cow: 284

llama: 330

humpback whale: 350

giraffe: 450

killer whale: 500

African elephant: 640

(one year) 400 days 500 days 600 days

Animal Senses

Our senses let us know what's going on in our environment. They allow us to communicate, keep us out of danger, and help us find food and shelter. Human senses include vision, hearing, taste, smell, and touch. Many animals have the same five senses, which are sometimes less and sometimes more sensitive than our own. Other creatures have senses that humans don't possess. These include echolocation (the ability to "see" with sound), infrared vision (seeing heat as well as light), and the ability to perceive electrical or magnetic fields.

The **diamondback rattlesnake** is a pit viper — it has heat-sensitive pits on its face that can detect the warm bodies of mice, rabbits, and other small mammals, allowing it to hunt in complete darkness.

LOOK

LISTEN

TOUCH

SMELL AND TASTE

HEAT, ELECTRICITY,
AND MAGNETISM

Look

For many animals, the eyes are the most important source of information about the world. All eyes work by reacting to light, but there are many different kinds of animal vision. The most basic eyes simply discern the difference between light and dark. Highly developed eyes detect motion, form images, and judge distances — abilities critical to the survival of many creatures, both predators and prey.

The compound eyes of the **honeybee** are composed of thousands of individual lenses, or facets, each producing a separate image.

The **jumping spider** has eight eyes. Four eyes on the sides of its head detect motion. Two others judge depth, while the two large eyes in the middle of its face form detailed images.

By moving its eyes independently, a **Jackson's chameleon** can look in two directions at once. As one eye searches for an insect to eat, the other watches for danger.

Despite its name, the **four-eyed fish** has only two eyes. But each eye contains two pupils. One watches above the surface for predators, and the other peers beneath the water, looking for insects and small fish to eat.

The **common frog** has good color vision and depth perception. But it doesn't seem to notice anything motionless. Surrounded by food that is not moving, this frog will starve to death.

The **kestrel** can see ultraviolet light — light that the human eye cannot detect. This bird's favorite food is a small rodent called a vole. As it moves about, the vole constantly dribbles pee, which reflects ultraviolet light. Flying overhead, the kestrel can simply follow a glowing trail to its prey.

Most deep-sea creatures cannot see red light. But the **stoplight loosejaw** can detect it, and it is this bizarre fish's secret weapon. A glowing red patch on its face illuminates its prey, which doesn't realize that it's been spotted until it's too late.

53

The **colossal squid,** the world's largest invertebrate, has eyes the size of a basketball. It lives deep in the ocean where no sunlight penetrates. But with its huge eyes it can see the faint glow made when a sperm whale, the squid's mortal enemy, disturbs the tiny bioluminescent creatures that live in the depths. This eye is shown at actual size.

Listen

Sound is actually a pattern of vibrations in the air, water, or earth. Many animals, including humans, have ears — specialized organs for detecting these vibrations. Other creatures "hear" through their antennae, their legs, or their skin. Many animals can detect sounds that are far outside the range of human hearing.

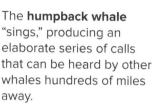

The **humpback whale** "sings," producing an elaborate series of calls that can be heard by other whales hundreds of miles away.

The **tenrec,** one of the few mammals capable of echolocation, navigates in the dark by making a series of clicking sounds and listening for the echoes.

The ears of the **tawny owl** are positioned at different heights on its head, helping the owl locate sounds in space. Its hearing is so sensitive that it can locate, in a fraction of a second, a mouse moving quietly beneath the snow.

By making rapid, high-pitched chirps and listening for the echoes, the **little brown bat** can flit about in total darkness, avoiding obstacles and catching flying insects.

The **dolphin** uses echolocation to find its prey. Though its hearing is not as sensitive as a bat's, it allows the dolphin to judge the size, distance, and speed of a fish or squid.

The **African elephant** generates low-frequency sounds that human ears cannot perceive. Other elephants can "hear" this rumbling with their trunk and feet from as much as six miles (10 kilometers) away.

The **cricket** can detect sound with ears located on its front legs.

Touch

Sight and hearing work at a distance, but the sense of touch is an animal's most direct connection with its surroundings. Some animals — especially those that live in an environment where it is a challenge to see or hear — rely on touch almost completely.

The **manatee** can feel at a distance — its body is covered with fine hairs that detect the presence of other animals through slight changes in water currents.

A **cat**'s whiskers can detect subtle movements of the air, allowing it to move about in the dark without bumping into anything.

Like many fish, **smelt** have a lateral line, a sense organ running down the sides of their bodies that is sensitive to touch and water pressure. The lateral line allows fish in a large school to swim in unison, turning at almost exactly the same moment.

The skin of the **channel catfish** is very sensitive to vibration, allowing this fish to detect danger or prey with its entire body.

The **starnose mole** spends its life underground, where it relies on its nose — and the 22 sensitive tentacles surrounding it — to find food and feel its way in the dark.

The **walrus** feeds on the sea floor, using its stiff but sensitive whiskers as probes. With its flexible lips it sucks clams, worms, and starfish from the mud.

Smell and taste

Unlike vision or hearing — senses that work by registering light or vibration — smell and taste detect chemicals in the air or water. These senses warn of nearby danger or poisonous substances. They can also help animals locate food or find a mate.

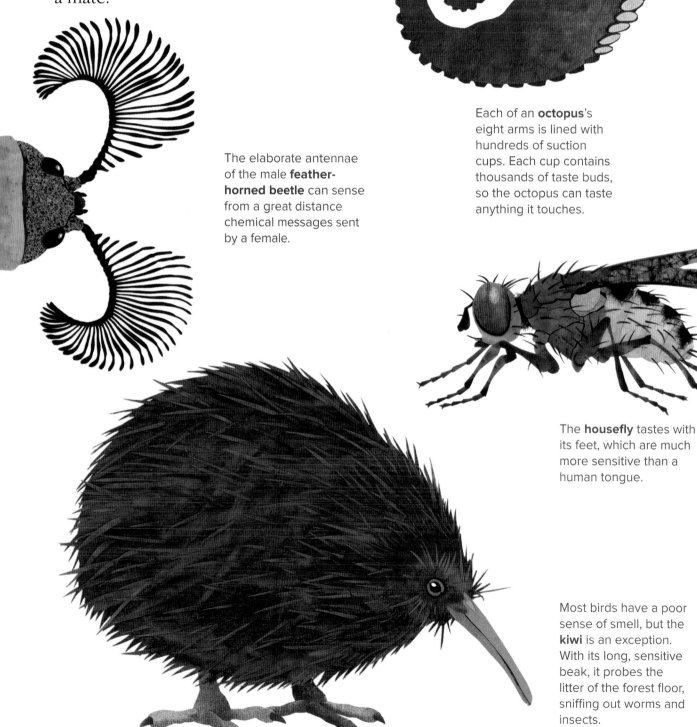

The elaborate antennae of the male **feather-horned beetle** can sense from a great distance chemical messages sent by a female.

Each of an **octopus**'s eight arms is lined with hundreds of suction cups. Each cup contains thousands of taste buds, so the octopus can taste anything it touches.

The **housefly** tastes with its feet, which are much more sensitive than a human tongue.

Most birds have a poor sense of smell, but the **kiwi** is an exception. With its long, sensitive beak, it probes the litter of the forest floor, sniffing out worms and insects.

The **bumblebee** tastes with its antennae, mouth parts, and forelegs. This helps it choose flowers that will be best for making honey.

As a **corn snake** flicks its tongue in and out, it collects odor molecules in the air and brings them to a special scent organ on the roof of its mouth. This organ has two openings, which is why the snake's tongue is forked.

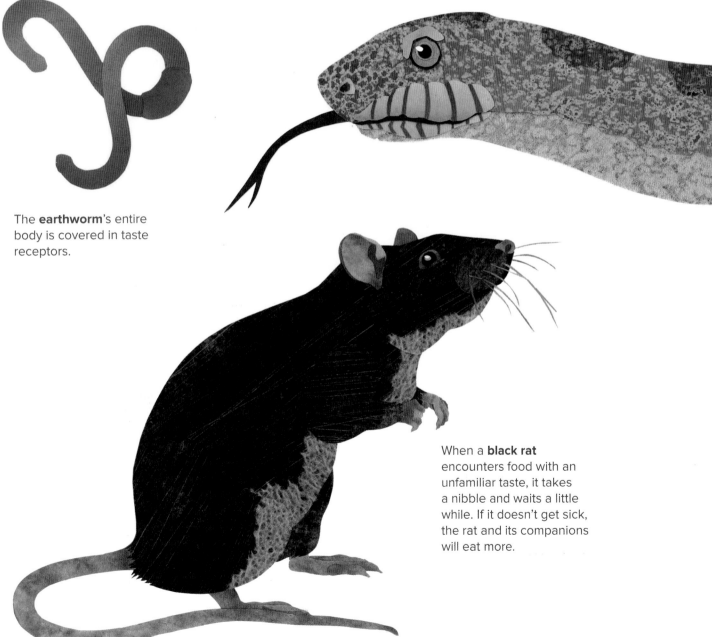

The **earthworm**'s entire body is covered in taste receptors.

When a **black rat** encounters food with an unfamiliar taste, it takes a nibble and waits a little while. If it doesn't get sick, the rat and its companions will eat more.

For most **dog** breeds, the primary sense is that of smell. A dog's nose is thousands — even millions — of times more sensitive than a human's.

Heat, electricity, and magnetism

It's hard to imagine "seeing" heat, or being able to recognize an animal by the faint electric field that it generates. It's even stranger to think of being able to find our way by using the earth's magnetic field. But there are animals that can do all of these things, and more.

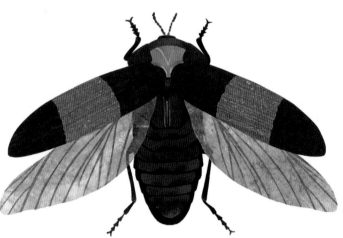

By generating a weak electric current, the **electric eel** can locate prey in the murky rivers where it lives. But when it's hunting — or if it's attacked — it can produce a jolt of electricity strong enough to stun a horse.

The **jewel beetle** can sense the heat of a forest fire from many miles away. Female beetles fly to the site of the fire and lay their eggs in charred wood, which is now free of predators.

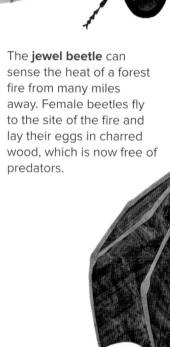

With its sensitive heat-detecting nose, a **vampire bat** can find the perfect place to suck blood from its prey — a spot where an animal's blood vessels are near the surface of its skin.

By orienting itself to the earth's magnetic field, the **naked mole rat** can find its way through an elaborate system of tunnels in total darkness.

The **great white shark** has dozens of spots on its snout that can sense the electric fields produced by fish and other prey.

A **platypus** probes a muddy river bottom, searching for insects and small animals to eat. On its bill are receptors sensitive to electricity that help it locate its prey.

How many eyes do animals have?

Animal	Number of eyes	Type of eye	
copepod	1		This tiny creature has just one eye in the center of its head.
rhinoceros	2		Almost all vertebrates posses two image-forming, or camera, eyes, each with a lens and retina.
tuatara	3		This lizard has a third, simple eye in the middle of its forehead.
sea star	5		Starfish have light-sensitive eyespots at the end of each arm. Most have five arms, but some have as many as 40.
wasp	5		Many insects have several simple eyes in addition to their two compound eyes.
jumping spider	8		This spider has four image-forming eyes and four simple eyes.
horseshoe crab	10		This ancient animal has two compound eyes on the top of its head and eight simple eyes scattered about its body.
scorpion	12		Some scorpions have five pairs of simple eyes in addition to their two compound eyes.
box jellyfish	24		Eight of this jellyfish's eyes can form images. The other 16 are light detectors.
scallop	100+		The blue-eyed scallop can have more than 100 image-forming eyes along the edge of its body.
giant clam	1000s		Hundreds — even thousands — of pinhole eyes cover the body of the giant clam.

Key

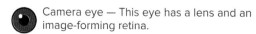

Camera eye — This eye has a lens and an image-forming retina.

Compound eye — This eye contains many individual lenses that form separate images.

Simple eye — This eye may or may not have a lens. Most simple eyes, including the pinhole eye, form crude images.

Eyespot — The simplest kind of eye. It can't form images, but it is sensitive to light.

Some animals that are sensitive to the earth's magnetic field

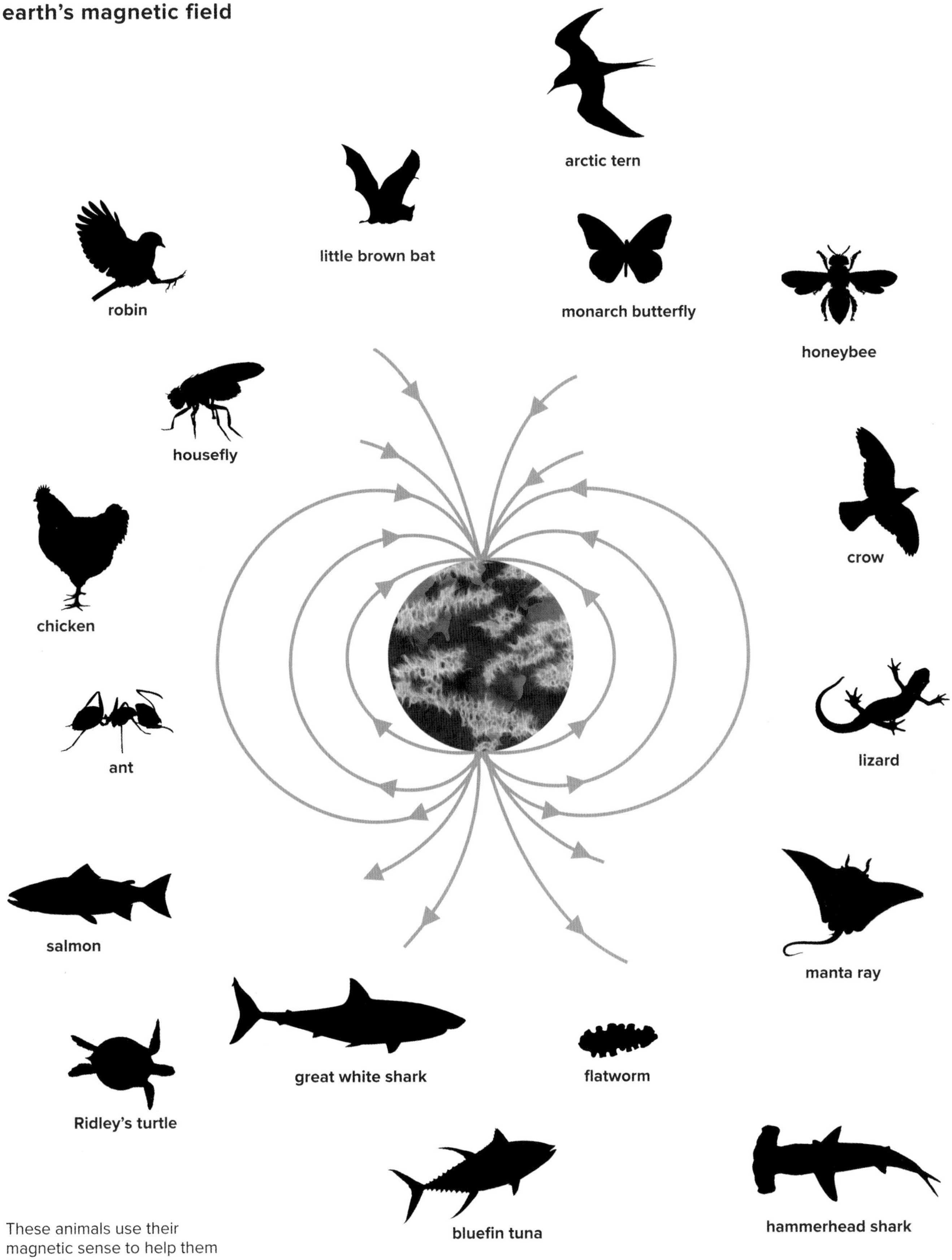

arctic tern

little brown bat

monarch butterfly

robin

honeybee

housefly

crow

chicken

lizard

ant

salmon

manta ray

Ridley's turtle

great white shark

flatworm

bluefin tuna

hammerhead shark

These animals use their magnetic sense to help them find their way, sometimes over great distances.

Predators

Animals have been killing and eating each other for hundreds of millions of years. Over that time, prey animals have devised clever ways of not getting eaten. Predators, in turn, have become stronger, faster, or smarter. This arms race is still going on. Predators get better at hunting while their prey finds new ways to escape, hide, or fight back. Plant-eaters have their own feeding strategies, but vegetation doesn't run away or actively fight back, so it's the meat-eaters who have come up with the most ingenious ways of getting enough to eat.

SPEEDY HUNTERS

AMBUSH!

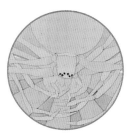

BLENDING IN

LURES

BEAKS, BARBS,
AND FANGS

SPECIAL WEAPONS
AND TACTICS

Lurking near the shore with just its eyes and nostrils above the water's surface, the **Nile crocodile** waits for an antelope or other animal to take a drink. Then, with a sudden thrust of its tail, it lunges onto the bank, grabs its victim, and pulls it back into the water.

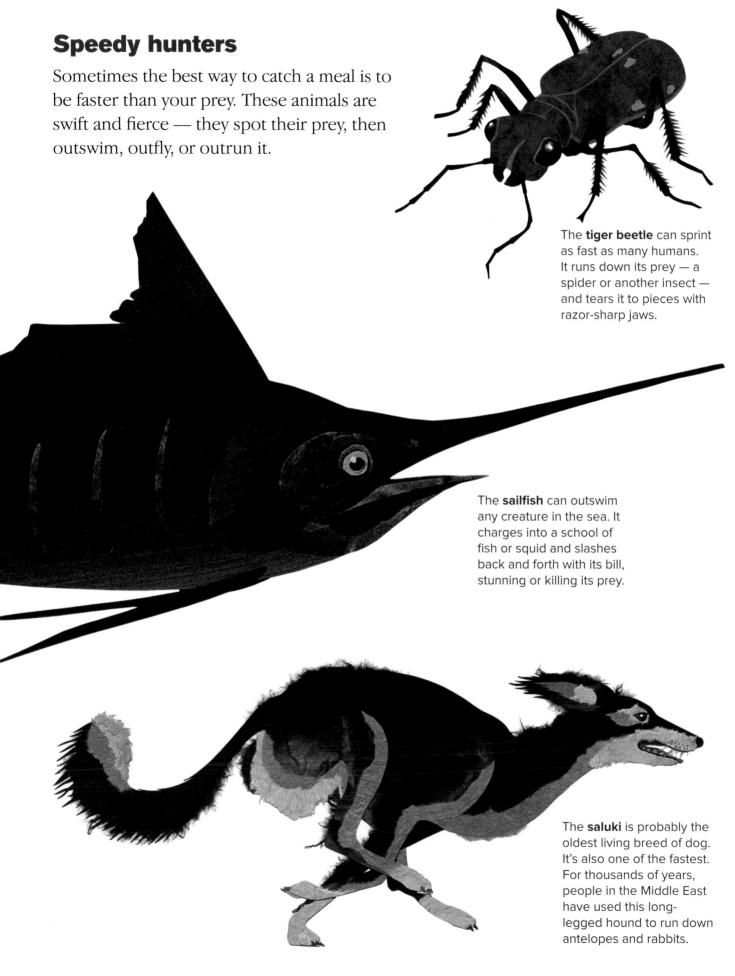

Speedy hunters

Sometimes the best way to catch a meal is to be faster than your prey. These animals are swift and fierce — they spot their prey, then outswim, outfly, or outrun it.

The **tiger beetle** can sprint as fast as many humans. It runs down its prey — a spider or another insect — and tears it to pieces with razor-sharp jaws.

The **sailfish** can outswim any creature in the sea. It charges into a school of fish or squid and slashes back and forth with its bill, stunning or killing its prey.

The **saluki** is probably the oldest living breed of dog. It's also one of the fastest. For thousands of years, people in the Middle East have used this long-legged hound to run down antelopes and rabbits.

The **dragonfly** can hover in place and fly faster than many birds. It hunts other flying insects, snatching them out of the air.

In level flight, the **spine-tailed swift** is the fastest bird in the world. Its speed and agility help it catch thousands of flying insects a day.

The **grizzly bear** may not look fast, but over short distances it can outsprint a horse. With this speed, it can even run down an elk or deer.

The **cheetah** is the fastest flat-out sprinter in the animal world. Over short distances, it can hit 70 miles (113 kilometers) per hour.

Ambush!

Chasing a meal requires a lot of energy and only pays off if a predator is fast enough to catch its prey. So some hunters take a different approach. They sneak up quietly or wait in hiding for a victim to get close enough, then suddenly grab or bite. This hunting method is known as "lurk and lunge."

A **trapdoor spider** waits, snug in its silk-lined burrow. It will pop out and grab any insect or small animal that wanders too close.

The **blue heron** steps carefully through shallow water, alert for a fish or frog. When it spots one, it stands as still as a statue until just the right moment. Then, with a sudden jab of its beak, it spears its prey.

The harmless-looking **grasshopper mouse** is actually an aggressive — and deadly — predator. It stalks, kills, and eats small animals, including other mice its own size.

Hovering motionless in the water, the **pike** waits for its quarry — a bird, frog, small mammal, or fish — to come near. Then it lunges forward and grabs its victim.

The deep-sea **black swallower** waits in the darkness for its meal to come to it. It swallows its prey whole, and it can gulp down a fish that is twice its own length.

The **Bengal tiger** prefers to attack from behind, getting as close as it can before leaping and killing its victim with a bite to the neck.

Blending in

A vine, a piece of coral, a flower — some predators look almost exactly like part of their environment. Often, these animals are also stealth or ambush hunters, stalking their prey or waiting until it gets close enough to pounce.

The **long-tailed weasel** is a fierce predator that can kill animals many times its own size. Its brown fur, which blends in with the rocks and leaves of the forest floor in summer, turns white in the winter. This helps it disappear in snowy landscapes.

The **green vine snake** appears to be a tangle of vegetation. It glides stealthily, feeding on birds, lizards, or small mammals.

The **stonefish** is found near tropical coral reefs. Resting on the sea floor, it looks like a lump of coral. If another fish gets too close, however, the stonefish can gulp it down in a split second.

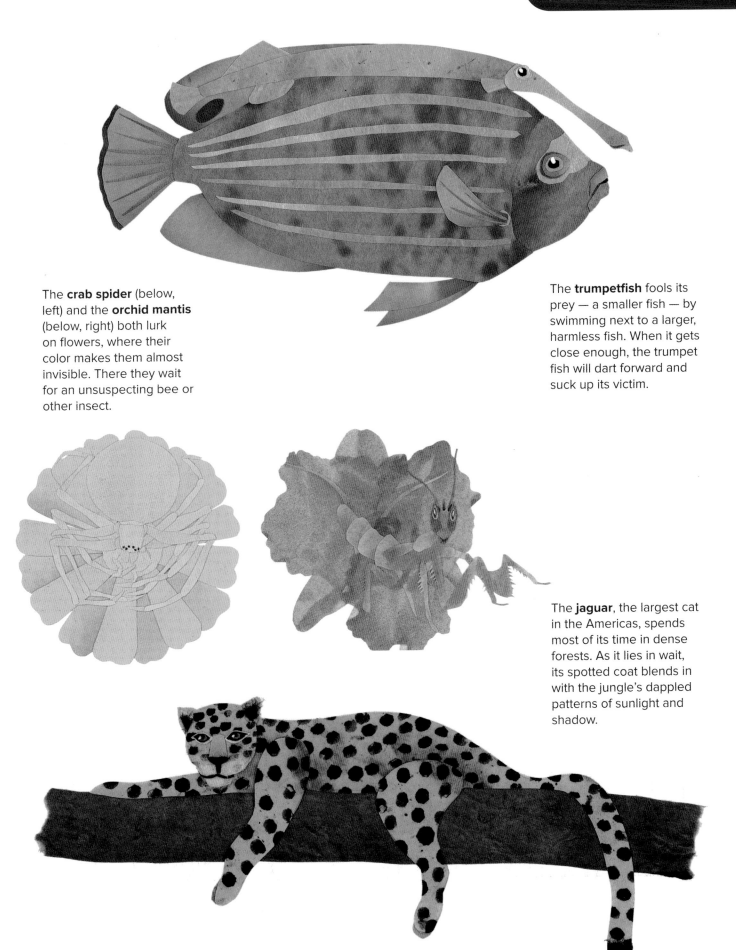

The **crab spider** (below, left) and the **orchid mantis** (below, right) both lurk on flowers, where their color makes them almost invisible. There they wait for an unsuspecting bee or other insect.

The **trumpetfish** fools its prey — a smaller fish — by swimming next to a larger, harmless fish. When it gets close enough, the trumpet fish will dart forward and suck up its victim.

The **jaguar**, the largest cat in the Americas, spends most of its time in dense forests. As it lies in wait, its spotted coat blends in with the jungle's dappled patterns of sunlight and shadow.

The **praying mantis** is a beautifully camouflaged ambush hunter. After waiting motionless for an insect, lizard, or other small animal to come within range, it shoots out its spine-covered legs and snags its prey.

Lures

These animals are ambush hunters with a twist: before they attack, they lure their prey into coming close. A body part, a light — even a sound — can be used as a lure.

A young **garter snake** dangles its tongue in a pond or stream. A curious fish investigates, only to become the snake's dinner.

An **alligator snapping turtle** rests on the bottom of a pond. It holds its mouth wide open and remains motionless except for a wriggling, worm-shaped growth on its tongue. When a fish tries to grab this "worm," the turtle's jaws snap shut.

The **margay** is a small wildcat that lives in the rainforest. It can imitate the cry of a baby monkey, pouncing when a concerned adult monkey comes to investigate.

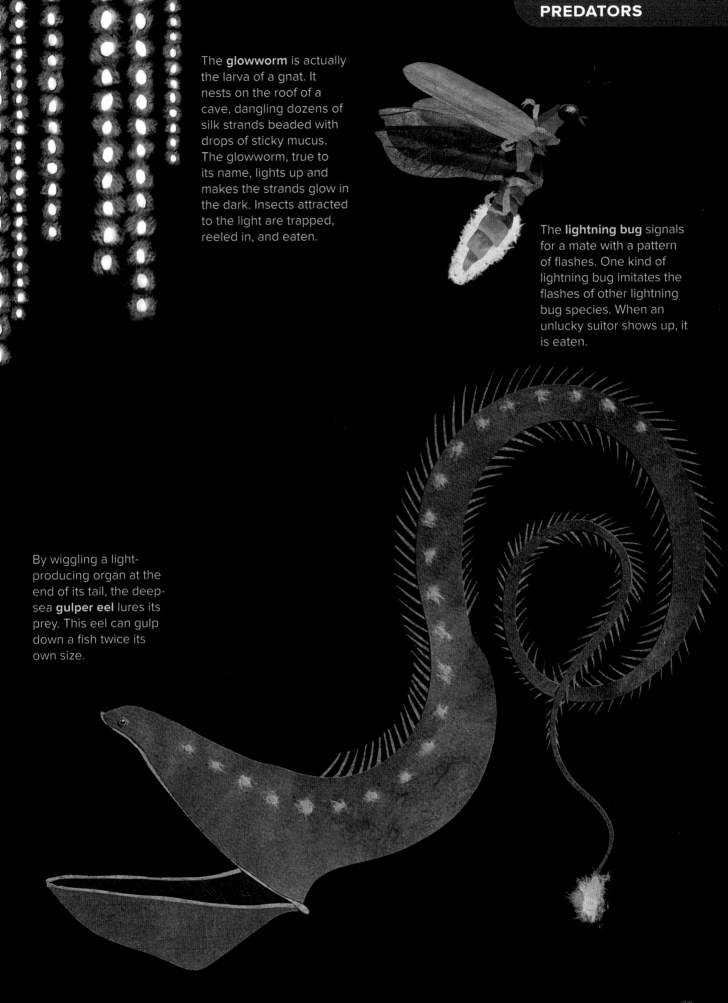

The **glowworm** is actually the larva of a gnat. It nests on the roof of a cave, dangling dozens of silk strands beaded with drops of sticky mucus. The glowworm, true to its name, lights up and makes the strands glow in the dark. Insects attracted to the light are trapped, reeled in, and eaten.

The **lightning bug** signals for a mate with a pattern of flashes. One kind of lightning bug imitates the flashes of other lightning bug species. When an unlucky suitor shows up, it is eaten.

By wiggling a light-producing organ at the end of its tail, the deep-sea **gulper eel** lures its prey. This eel can gulp down a fish twice its own size.

Beaks, barbs, and fangs

The skin or flesh of poisonous animals contains toxins that are commonly used as a defense. The animals shown here, however, are venomous — they deliver their poison with a bite or sting, using it to paralyze or kill their prey.

The **blue-ringed octopus** is one of the most venomous animals on earth. It uses its toxin — injected with a razor-sharp beak — to kill the crabs, shrimp, and fish it eats.

The venom of the **sea krait** may be the deadliest of any snake's. This reptile spends its life in the ocean, feeding on eels, fish, and other marine creatures.

The **box jellyfish,** also known as the sea wasp, causes more human deaths than any other sea creature. Its venom kills fish and shrimp so quickly that they don't have a chance to struggle and damage the jellyfish's delicate tentacles.

The **geographic cone snail** hunts fish and shrimp with a venomous barb that it can throw like a harpoon. Unlucky human beachcombers have picked up this beautiful shell only to receive a fatal dose of toxin.

The **assassin bug** stalks its prey and spears it with a jab of its venomous, swordlike "beak."

Along with the Gila monster, the **Mexican beaded lizard** is one of two venomous lizards that live in North America. It preys on small mammals, nesting birds, and eggs.

The **solenodon** is a mammal that resembles a large shrew. It immobilizes its prey — insects, worms, and small animals — with poisonous saliva.

Special weapons and tactics

Many predators rely on their claws and fangs when they hunt. Other animals are more inventive, using specially adapted body parts to help them catch, kill, and eat their prey.

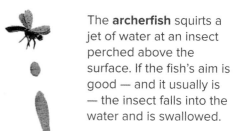

The **archerfish** squirts a jet of water at an insect perched above the surface. If the fish's aim is good — and it usually is — the insect falls into the water and is swallowed.

To get to the soft flesh of a clam, a **herring gull** picks it up in its beak, carries it high into the air, and drops it repeatedly on rocks — or a parking lot — until its shell shatters.

The **mantis shrimp** has a hard, club-shaped foot that delivers a kick with enough force to shatter an oyster's shell or smash a crab into pieces. This blow has even been known to break the glass wall of an aquarium.

The female **bolas spider** produces a scent that imitates a moth's chemical messages. When a moth responds, the spider swings a thread with a blob of sticky silk at one end, capturing the insect.

Circling beneath a school of fish, a pod of **dolphins** blows out a curtain of air bubbles. The fish crowd together inside this bubble "net," and the dolphins plunge straight through them, snapping up fish left and right.

The **crucifix toad** stores captured insects on its sticky, mucus-covered skin. The toad regularly sheds its skin — pulling it off over its head like a sweater — and eats it, bugs and all.

A forest food web

This food web shows some of the interactions — who eats whom — in an Asian forest. Not all of the interactions between predators and prey are shown, but this diagram does hint at how complex these relationships can be.

bat

antelope

heron

dragonfly

spider

rabbit

frog

grasshopper

shrew

cricket

dead animal

snake

eagle

gibbon

kingfisher

jackal

tiger

fish

lizard

fly

vulture

raccoon

Defenses

There are a few creatures so big or so fierce that no other animal tries to eat them. But most animals are in constant danger of becoming another creature's meal. Predators have evolved a wide variety of ways to catch and kill their prey, but their potential victims have come up with equally impressive survival strategies.

GETTING AWAY

HIDING IN PLAIN SIGHT

COPYCATS

PROTECTIVE POISON

ARMOR AND SPINES

Clinging to a dried-up branch, the **satanic leaf-tailed gecko** appears to be part of a dead plant. It even has notches in its tail that make it look like a decaying leaf.

BODILY FLUIDS

SURPRISE!

FIGHTING BACK

WORKING TOGETHER

Getting away

One of the best ways to avoid predators is to never let them get close. Some animals are fast and can simply outrun danger. Others have perfected more unusual ways of escaping.

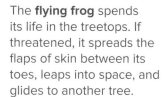

The **flying frog** spends its life in the treetops. If threatened, it spreads the flaps of skin between its toes, leaps into space, and glides to another tree.

The **pronghorn antelope** is the fastest land animal in North America — much faster than any predator on this continent. Its speed is left over from its ancestors' days of outrunning lions and cheetahs, swift predators that roamed the Americas until about 11,000 years ago.

The **green basilisk lizard** is also known as the Jesus Christ lizard. To escape danger, it drops from a tree branch and sprints across the water's surface.

Unlike most shellfish, the **flame scallop** can move quickly. To get away from a hungry starfish, it squirts water from its shell and jets backwards.

To escape danger, the **mother-of-pearl moth caterpillar** curls itself into the shape of a wheel, hurls itself backwards, and rolls away.

Pursued by a fish, a **Japanese flying squid** bursts from the surface and soars through the air. It reenters the water as much as 150 feet (46 meters) away.

The **pebble toad** lives on rocky cliff faces. When danger is near, it curls into a ball, lets go, and tumbles down the slope. To a predator, the toad looks like a pebble bouncing down the mountainside.

Hiding in plain sight

Blending in is a good way to hide from birds, fish, and other predators — especially those that rely on their eyesight to find their prey.

The **three-toed sloth** spends its life in the trees of the rainforest. Its damp fur is home to a kind of algae (*al-jee*), a tiny single-celled plant. The algae gives the sloth's coat a green tint, which makes it difficult to spot as it dangles among the foliage.

The body of the **glass frog** is transparent. When it clings to a leaf, this little frog almost seems to disappear.

The deep-ocean **hatchet fish** has luminous patches on its belly that adjust in brightness to match the faint illumination coming from the surface. This makes the fish almost impossible to spot when viewed from below.

The brightly colored **eyelash viper** looks as if it would be hard to miss. Coiled among the colorful yellow flowers and fruit of the jungle, however, it is well camouflaged.

The **decorator crab** attaches bits of sponge, seaweed, and debris to its shell. When it holds still, it looks like a piece of the sea floor.

The coat of a baby **tapir** is patterned with spots and stripes. These markings help the tapir fade into the dappled shadows of its forest home.

Copycats

Animal mimics don't try to hide. Instead, they pretend to be something they are not: a dangerous animal, part of a plant, or something unappetizing to even the hungriest predator.

Two spots on the tail of the **spicebush swallowtail butterfly caterpillar** make it easy for a bird to mistake this insect for the head of a snake.

The **burrowing owl** chick lives in an underground nest. When threatened by a fox or weasel, it can imitate the sound of a rattlesnake's warning rattle.

The **viceroy butterfly** (top) closely resembles the **monarch butterfly** (bottom). Both are poisonous and bad-tasting. By mimicking each other, they make it more likely that a predator will know from experience that neither of them is good to eat.

The **ant beetle** looks and smells like an ant. It lives in an ant nest, and the ants, believing it's one of them, feed and protect it.

As it hovers almost motionless in the water, the **leafy seadragon** appears to be a piece of seaweed.

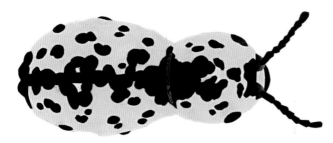

When it tucks its legs beneath its body, there is a good chance that the **ironclad beetle** will be mistaken for a pile of bird droppings.

The **pootoo** is active at night. During the day, this bird pretends to be part of a dead tree stump. Its eyes are almost — but not quite — closed, so it can watch for danger.

Protective poison

Many animals use toxins, or poisons, for self-defense. Some creatures produce their own toxins. Others acquire them from their diet or environment.

The bright color of the **Malaysian cherry-red centipede** warns predators that it is poisonous.

The **cane toad** is a gentle insect eater. It protects itself with two large sacs of poison on its neck. If pressed, these pouches expel a deadly toxin.

The male **platypus** is one of the few venomous mammals. It has poisonous spurs on its back legs.

The **weeverfish** buries itself in the sand, popping out to grab smaller fish. Poisonous spines on its back protect it against its own predators.

The skin and feathers of the **hooded pitohui** contain a deadly poison, acquired from the beetles that this bird feeds on.

As it feeds on ants and centipedes, the **poison dart frog** accumulates insect toxins in its skin. One of these tiny frogs contains enough poison to kill 20 people.

The **boxer crab** defends itself by plucking poisonous anemones from the sea floor and waving them like boxing gloves in the face of an attacker.

The **slow loris** is the only poisonous primate. When threatened, it licks venom glands on its elbows, then bites its attacker, chewing toxic saliva into the wound.

Armor and spines

More than 500 million years ago, animals living in the oceans developed hard shells to protect against predators. Since then, all sorts of animals have evolved scales, spines, shells, and other ways of shielding their bodies from attack.

Holding its tail in its mouth, the **armadillo lizard** forms a spiny, armored wheel. In this position, the lizard's soft belly is protected.

The **nautilus,** a creature that looks like a squid with a shell, has changed very little in 500 million years.

The **tortoise beetle** — like its larger, reptilian namesake — can tuck its legs beneath its shell for protection.

The **porcupine**'s quills cannot be thrown, as is sometimes believed, but they detach easily. Once lodged in an attacker's flesh, a quill's barbed tip makes it difficult to remove.

The **spiny orb web spider** gets its name from the hard, sharp spines on its body and the circular shape of its web. Its spines makes it less appetizing to a bird or other predator.

The **pangolin,** also known as the scaly anteater, is protected by sharp-edged, overlapping scales. It rolls itself into an armored ball when threatened.

By inflating its body with water, the **pufferfish** turns itself into a prickly ball and becomes almost impossible for a larger fish to swallow.

The thick, tough hide of the **Indian rhinoceros** is arranged in overlapping segments that form a full suit of armor.

97

Bodily fluids

Being poisonous or tasting terrible is a common protection in the animal world. These animals, however, have taken chemical defense to another level. Rather than waiting for predators to take a bite — which could be fatal for them — they cover themselves in protective substances or hurl, squirt, or spray them onto an attacker.

By forcing air through its own blood, the **African foam grasshopper** blankets itself in a protective toxic froth.

The **bombardier beetle** sprays a jet of boiling hot, noxious liquid from its rear end into the face of a predator.

Nesting **European roller** chicks respond to a threat by vomiting all over themselves. This makes them unappetizing as prey.

Like all cobras, the **red spitting cobra** can subdue its prey with a venomous bite. But this snake also defends itself by spitting its poison. It aims for the eyes, and its toxin can cause permanent blindness.

A **horned lizard** startles an attacker by expelling blood from its eyes. The blood, which can be squirted several feet, tastes bad to most animals.

When assaulted by another bird, the **fulmar gull** chick hurls the oily contents of its stomach onto its attacker. The sticky vomit glues the larger bird's feathers together, often resulting in its death.

The bioluminescent **deep-sea shrimp** ejects a blob of sticky, glowing goo when an attacker gets close. The predator, lit up and unable to hide in the darkness, is now likely to become a victim itself.

A **Malaysian ant** soldier, also known as an exploding ant, carries large toxin sacs on the sides of its body. If its colony is threatened, the ant sacrifices itself by violently contracting its muscles, rupturing the sacs and spraying sticky poison in all directions. Attackers are covered in deadly goo and killed or immobilized.

Surprise!

Using sound, color, special markings, or a sudden movement to startle an attacker can be an effective defense. It may scare away a predator or distract it long enough to allow its potential victim to escape.

The **armadillo** usually relies on its armor plating for protection. But if it doesn't have time to roll into a ball, it has another trick. It leaps several feet straight up into the air, startling a coyote or other predator.

When threatened, the **Budgett's frog** stands on tiptoe and lets out a shrill scream.

The **blue-winged grasshopper** is a dull brown color until it spreads its wings, suddenly revealing two bright blue patches. This flash of color can startle a bird or other predator.

The **frilled lizard** has loose folds of skin around its neck. When frightened, it opens its bright pink mouth and spreads its frill, making it appear much larger.

Many predators won't eat animals that are not alive. The **hog-nosed snake** plays dead by rolling over, sticking out its tongue, and letting a little blood run out of its mouth. It can even release a fluid from its rear end that smells like a dead animal.

The **red-eyed tree frog** sleeps during the day. If it's disturbed, its eyes spring open. The sudden appearance of two bright red orbs can frighten a predator.

The **tiger moth** is poisonous and its bright red underwings can startle an attacker. Its most interesting defense, however, is its ability to jam the hunting sonar of bats by producing its own high-pitched sounds.

The **blue-tailed skink** can detach its tail when danger threatens. The bright blue tail twitches and wriggles, drawing a predator's attention while the lizard makes its escape.

Fighting back

Prey animals try to avoid being seen, heard, or smelled by predators. If they can't avoid detection, most would rather run away than stand and fight. But sometimes encounters with an enemy are unavoidable, and putting up a battle is the only option.

The **yellow tang** carries two razor-sharp spines folded against its body. If it is attacked, it extends the spines and whips its tail back and forth. This slashing action can injure or kill a predator.

The unpredictable and aggressive **cape buffalo** is one of the most dangerous animals in Africa. Its horns and hooves are lethal weapons, giving even a hungry lion pause.

The **Chilean rose tarantula** has a venomous bite. It also has another, more unusual form of defense. With a leg, it flicks fine hairs from its body. They can lodge in an attacker's skin or eyes, causing painful irritation.

The **stingray** can thrust the long, poisonous barb at the base of its tail into the body of an attacker.

When it has to defend itself, the **hairy frog** breaks the bones in its own feet. Sharp bone fragments pierce the frog's skin and serve as claws to fend off predators.

The **warthog** has two pairs of tusks. The lower pair grinds against the upper pair every time the warthog opens and closes its mouth, making them razor-sharp. The tusks are used both to dig up food and as defensive weapons.

The **cassowary** is a large flightless bird. If cornered, it can deliver a kick with its clawed foot that is powerful enough to cave in a person's chest.

Working together

Some animals band together to overwhelm predators with strength of numbers. Others cooperate with an animal of a different species to discourage their enemies.

The **hermit crab** makes its home in an abandoned mollusk shell, on which it sometimes places a **sea anemone.** The anemone's poisonous tentacles protect the crab. In return, the anemone gets scraps from the crab's meals.

When a hornet invades their hive, hundreds of **Japanese honeybees** cluster in a tight ball around the much larger intruder. They vibrate their bodies frantically, producing enough heat to cook the hornet to death.

Peering from the burrow of a **blind shrimp,** a **goby** checks for danger. If the coast is clear, it will lead the shrimp out to search for food. In return for acting as lookout, the little fish gets to share the shrimp's home.

If a hawk approaches a **crow**'s nest and threatens its young, several crows join forces to drive it away. This behavior is called mobbing.

The **clownfish** takes shelter among the poison tentacles of a **giant green anemone.** It becomes immune to its own anemone's toxin, but the little fish would be killed if it swam into a different anemone.

The **rufous woodpecker** makes a hole in a black ant nest and lays her eggs inside. The ants don't attack her, the eggs, or the newly hatched chicks. In return, the mother bird defends the ants and their nest against predators.

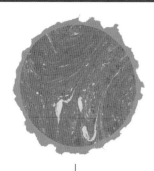

An ecological pryamid

This food pyramid shows one food chain on land and another in the ocean. Animals typically eat the organisms at the level below them on the pyramid. Plants and algae at the base of the pyramid convert solar energy to food. Except for a few organisms that live near volcanic vents in the sea, all life on earth gets its energy directly or indirectly from the sun.

On land, plants combine sunlight and carbon dioxide, a gas, to produce food. This process is called photosynthesis.

Apex predators

These animals have no natural enemies in their habitat (though many are threatened by humans). They eat primary and secondary consumers.

Secondary consumers

These animals are carnivores. They eat primary consumers.

Primary consumers

These animals are herbivores. They eat producers.

Producers

These organisms — plants, algae, and bacteria — convert the sun's energy directly to food.

In the oceans, the main food producer is algae, both single-celled organisms (shown here greatly enlarged) and seaweed, another form of algae.

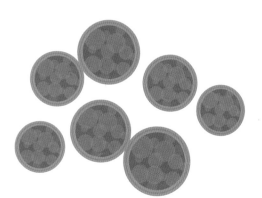

Animal Extremes

For some animals, being gigantic is a good survival strategy. Others have taken a different approach and are almost to small for us to see. Here, along with these big and little creatures, are some of the longest, loudest, oldest, hardiest, and most dangerous animals.

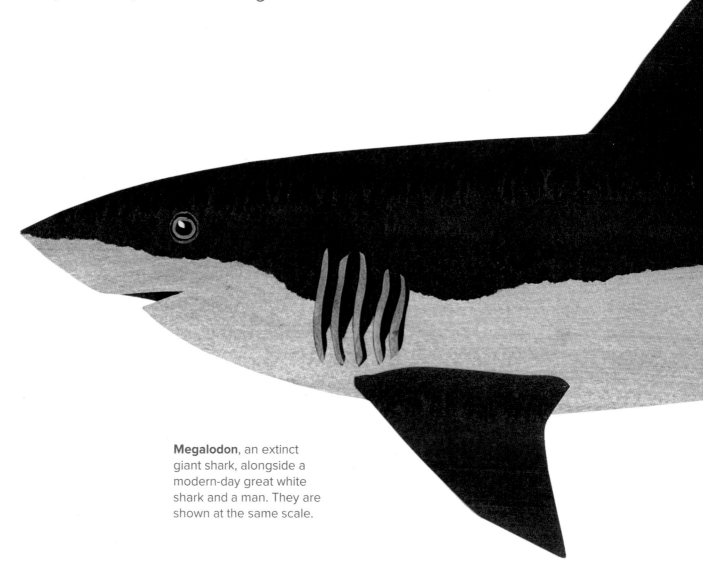

Megalodon, an extinct giant shark, alongside a modern-day great white shark and a man. They are shown at the same scale.

THE BIGGEST EVER

PREHISTORIC GIANTS

BIG AND LITTLE

ACTUAL SIZE

IT'S A SMALL WORLD

LONGEST

SOUNDING OFF

LIFE SPANS

HOTTEST, COLDEST,
HIGHEST, DEEPEST

DEADLIEST
TO HUMANS

The biggest ever

We don't know for sure why some dinosaurs grew so large. It might have had to do with a warm climate and a surplus of plant food. Perhaps a warm body temperature and light, hollow bones allowed them to become giants. Whatever the reason, we know that dinosaurs were, by far, the largest animals to ever live on land. But in the sea, where an animal's weight is supported by the water, creatures even bigger than the biggest dinosaur can still be found.

Spinosaurus lived 100 million years ago. It was 50 feet (15 meters) long and fed on fish. It may have been the largest predatory dinosaur — and the largest meat-eater to ever live on land.

The **blue whale,** the largest animal to ever live, is more than twice as heavy as the giant dinosaur above.

It lived 95 million years ago. And at 100 feet (30½ meters) in length, plant-eating *Argentinosaurus* (**ahr**-*gen*-**teen**-*uh*-**sawr**-*us*) is the current record holder for dinosaur size. Claims have been made for larger dinosaurs, but so far there is not enough fossil evidence to prove their existence.

All of these animals — along with an adult human — are pictured at the same scale.

The **African elephant,** the largest living land animal, stands 13 feet (4 meters) tall at the shoulder.

Prehistoric giants: amphibians and reptiles

Before the age of dinosaurs, giant amphibians were the top predators on land. Millions of years later, when dinosaurs assumed that role, huge reptiles dominated the air and the sea.

Around 260 million years ago amphibians ruled the land. The largest of them all was *Prionosuchus* (*pri-**ahn**-o-**soo**-kus*), a 30-foot (9-meter)-long meat-eater.

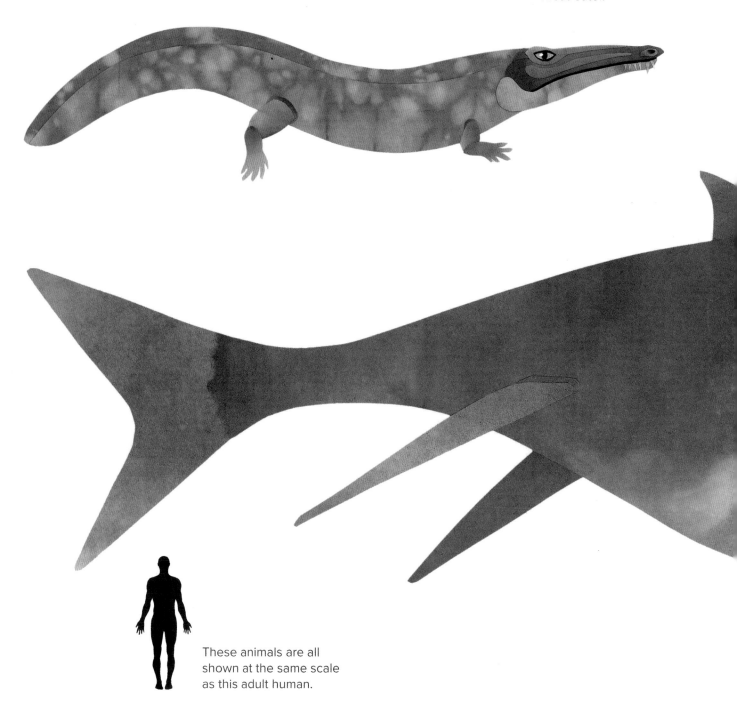

These animals are all shown at the same scale as this adult human.

Quetzalcoatlus (***kwet***-*zal-koh-**at**-lus*) may have been the biggest animal to ever take to the skies. It had a wingspan of 36 feet (11 meters). It lived near the end of the dinosaur age, about 68 million years ago.

Prehistoric reptiles that lived in the ocean could reach enormous sizes. *Shastasaurus* (***shass***-*tah-**sore**-us*) was almost 70 feet (21 meters) long. It lived about 210 million years ago and hunted fish and squid.

Prehistoric giants: birds and mammals

About 65 million years ago the last of the dinosaurs became extinct. In the millions of years that followed, birds and mammals grew larger. They filled roles in the ecosystem such as top predator and giant grazing animal — roles that dinosaurs had once played.

Indricotherium (*in-dre-ko-thir-e-um*) was a herbivore that lived in what is now Asia about 30 million years ago. At four times the weight of an African elephant, it was the largest mammal to ever live on land.

Two million years ago, this giant **rat** lived in South America. It weighed 2,200 pounds (1,000 kilograms) — as much as a large bull.

The **elephant bird** stood 10 feet (3 meters) tall and was one of the largest birds of all time. This giant died out about 300 years ago.

Elasmotherium (*e-las-mo-**ther**-e-um*) was a rhinoceros the size of an elephant that lived in Europe and Asia until about 50,000 years ago. It used its enormous horn for defense and for digging up plants and roots.

These animals are shown at the same scale as this adult human.

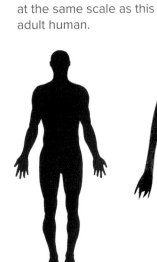

117

Big and little

Animals that are closely related may look similar and behave in similar ways but still vary enormously in size. This allows them to live in different habitats and hunt prey of different sizes.

The stealth, speed, and keen senses of the **Siberian tiger** and the **housecat** — shown here at the same scale — make them almost perfect predators.

The **leatherback sea turtle,** the largest of all turtles, weighs as much as a small car. With its enormous flippers, it glides through the ocean as it feeds on jellyfish. The much smaller **spotted turtle,** shown at the same scale, has a similar lifestyle, paddling through ponds and streams and feeding on worms and insects.

The **reticulated python** is the longest snake in the world. It has been reliably measured at 25 feet (7½ meters) in length, though there are many unconfirmed reports of longer snakes. The much smaller **ring-necked snake** also kills its prey by squeezing it to death. But unlike the python, which has no venom, the smaller snake also injects a weak toxin into its victims.

Actual size

The animals — or parts of animals — on the next eight pages are shown life-size.

The **Goliath birdeater tarantula** is big enough to catch and eat birds and small mammals.

The **titan beetle** has the longest body of any beetle. Its jaws are powerful enough to snap a pencil in half.

This two-foot (61-centimeter) tongue — one of the longest in the animal world — is the perfect tool for slurping up ants and termites. It belongs to a **giant anteater.**

Here is the **Siberian tiger** at actual size. It is the biggest of the big cats.

The **Atlas moth** is so large that it is often mistaken for a bird.

The **gorilla** is the largest primate. Clinging to its hand is a **pygmy mouse lemur,** the smallest of the primates.

131

It's a small world.

Being small can offer real advantages to an animal. It doesn't need as much food as a big animal, and it's easier to hide from predators. But there are limits to how tiny an animal can become. Birds and mammals must be large enough to keep their body warm. Cold-blooded animals — reptiles, amphibians, and fish — can be smaller, but their body has to be big enough to contain a heart, a brain, and other organs. Some invertebrates are much tinier, but they are still limited by the minimum number of cells their bodies need to function.

The **bumblebee bat** is a competitor for the title of smallest mammal. It weighs less than a Ping-Pong ball.

The **Etruscan shrew** weighs less than the bumblebee bat, but its body is a little longer. It must eat almost constantly — if it goes an hour without food, it can starve to death.

The **bee hummingbird** is the smallest bird. Its body is not much larger than that of a bumblebee.

These animals are shown life-size.

The **thread snake** is the smallest known species of snake, with a body the thickness of a pencil lead.

The tiny **Amau frog** was discovered in the jungles of New Guinea in 2012. It now holds the title of world's smallest vertebrate — the smallest animal with a backbone.

Paedocypris (*pee-do-kip-ris*) is the world's smallet fish. It was considered the smallest vertebrate until the discovery of the Amau frog.

The smallest known spider is the *Patu digua* of South America. It is shown below, greatly enlarged, and above (inside the circle) at actual size.

Rotifers are also called wheel animals because of the rotating hairlike structures they use to move through the water. They are the smallest of all animals. The rotifer shown here, *euchlanis*, is about half the size of the period at the end of this sentence. Though tiny, it has eyes, a brain, and a digestive system.

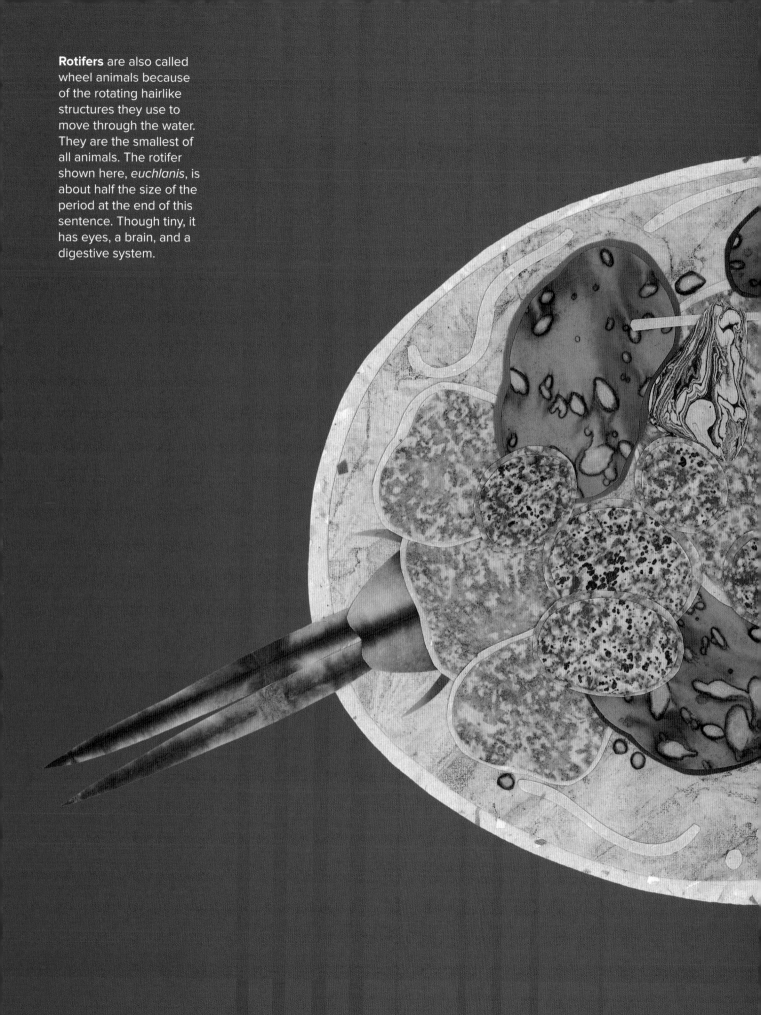

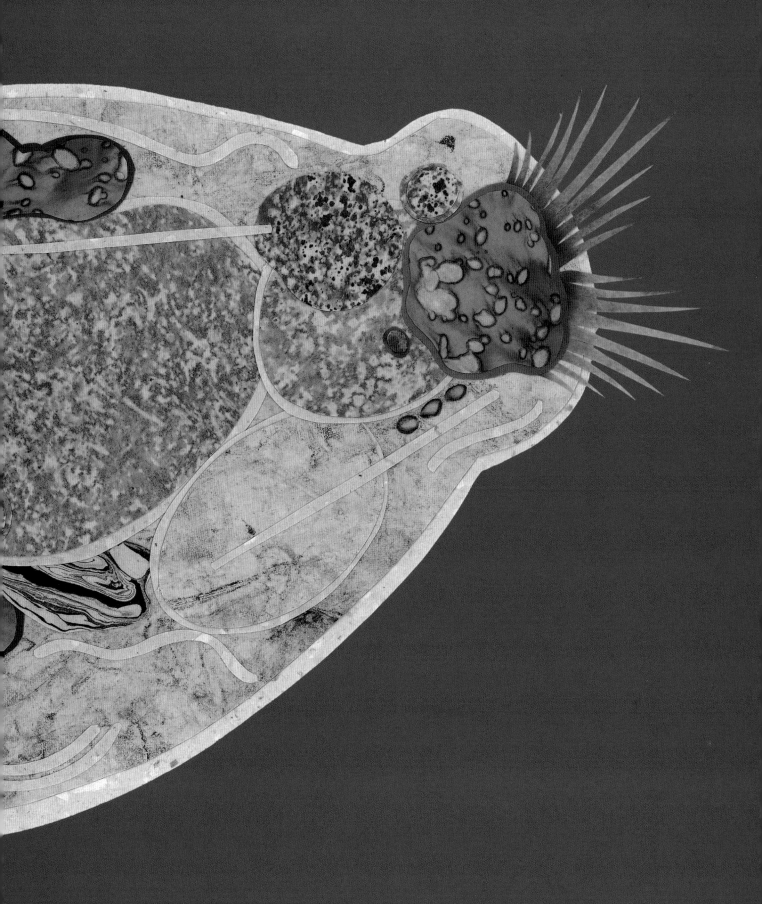

Longest

There is more than one way to judge an animal's size. We can measure its weight or its height. Or, as with the record-holding creatures on these pages, we can assess their length or the length of some of their body parts.

The world's longest animal, the **giant ribbon worm,** lives on the ocean floor. Some of these worms reach 180 feet (55 meters) in length, but may be no thicker than your finger.

The **lion's mane jellyfish** trails stinging tentacles 120 feet (36½ meters) long as it drifts through the water.

The world's longest tooth belongs to the male **narwhal,** a kind of whale. It uses this ten-foot (3-meter)-long tusk in mating battles with other males.

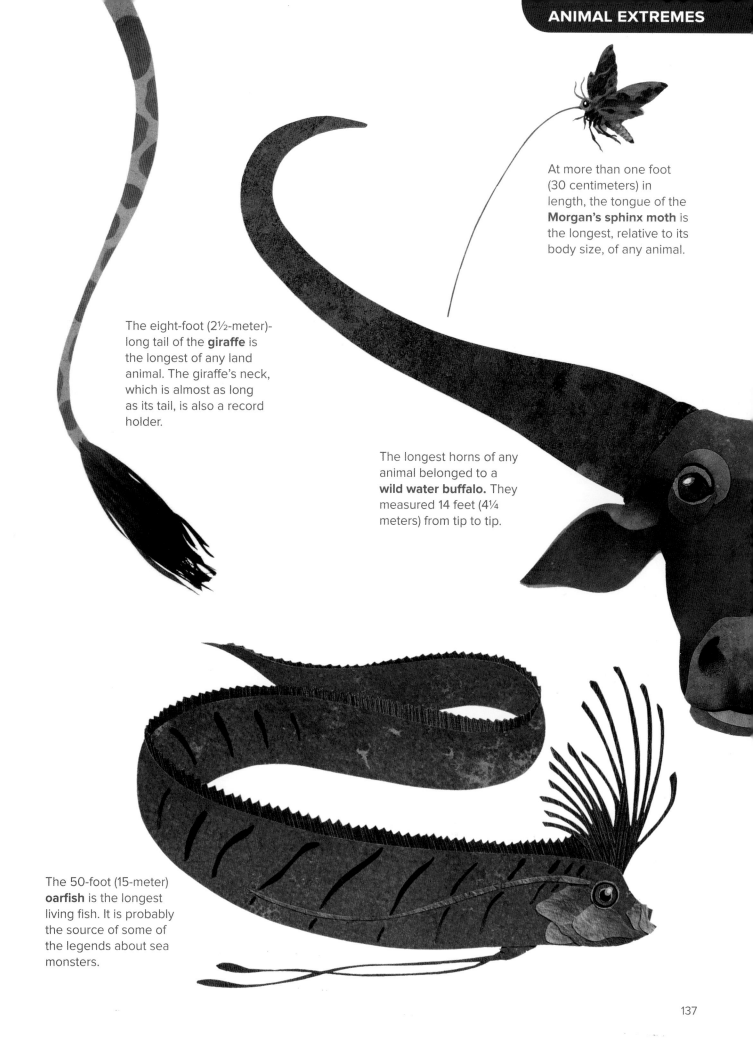

At more than one foot (30 centimeters) in length, the tongue of the **Morgan's sphinx moth** is the longest, relative to its body size, of any animal.

The eight-foot (2½-meter)-long tail of the **giraffe** is the longest of any land animal. The giraffe's neck, which is almost as long as its tail, is also a record holder.

The longest horns of any animal belonged to a **wild water buffalo.** They measured 14 feet (4¼ meters) from tip to tip.

The 50-foot (15-meter) **oarfish** is the longest living fish. It is probably the source of some of the legends about sea monsters.

Sounding off

Many animals use sound to communicate, often when they are signaling a mate. A few employ sound as a weapon. The creatures shown here make some of the loudest sounds in the animal world.

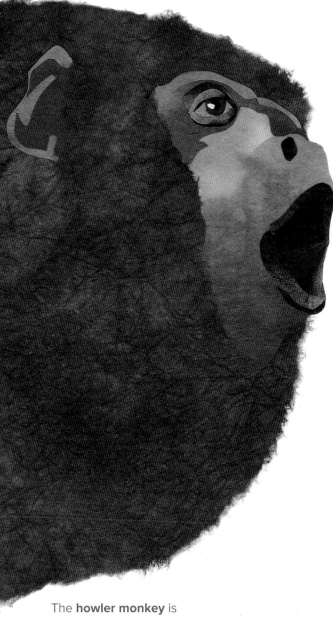

The **kakapo** is a flightless parrot that is active at night. To attract a female, the male produces a powerful booming sound, often for hours at a time.

Mole crickets live in underground tunnels. At mating time, a male digs a special tunnel with two openings. Then he climbs inside and sings for a female. The tunnel acts as an amplifier, carrying his song for a great distance.

The **howler monkey** is the loudest land animal. A troop of howlers making their guttural calls can be heard for miles around.

If a male **cicada** is held close to a person's ear, the rapid clicking song it produces is loud enough to cause permanent hearing loss. When thousands of cicadas sing together, the noise can be almost unbearable.

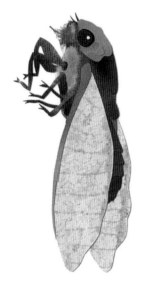

The **pistol shrimp,** also known as a snapping shrimp, hunts with sound. It waits until a small fish gets close, then snaps shut a special claw. This produces a noise so loud that the shock wave created stuns or kills its prey.

The **blue whale** is the loudest animal on earth. Its call is much louder than the sound of a jet engine, and can be heard for hundreds of miles underwater.

Life spans

Some animals live long, slow lives, surviving for many human lifetimes. Others speed through life, living as adults for only a few minutes. Here are a few of the creatures that have unusually long or short life spans.

Galápagos tortoise
175 years

tubeworm
170 years

bowhead whale
200 years

sea urchin
200 years

koi
226 years

quahog clam
410 years

giant barrel sponge
2,300 years

mayfly
30 minutes to 24 hours

housefly
3 weeks

European water vole
5 months

Hottest, coldest, highest, deepest

Animals have adapted to some of the most extreme conditions on earth. Living in a place where few other creatures can survive offers some benefits to an animal that can withstand the challenges of the environment. It may face less competition for food and be in less danger from predators.

The **kangaroo rat** is at home in the desert. It can live its entire life without taking a drink, getting all the moisture it needs from its diet of seeds.

The **Pompeii worm** lives near deep-sea volcanic vents. It thrives in water as hot as 176° F (80° C), a temperature that would cook most animals.

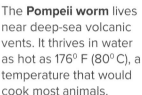

Most cold-blooded animals will die if their body gets too cold. The **wood frog,** however, can freeze solid in the winter, sitting on the forest floor like a stone. In the spring it will thaw out and hop away.

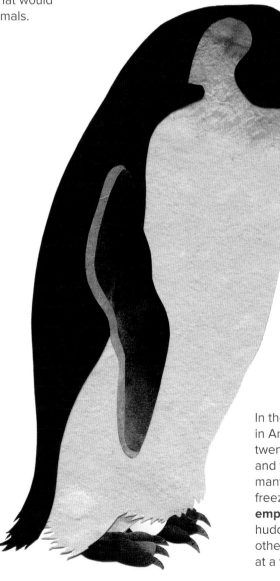

In the middle of the winter in Antarctica, it's dark twenty-four hours a day and the temperature is many degrees below freezing. But the male **emperor penguin** endures, huddling on the ice with other penguins for months at a time.

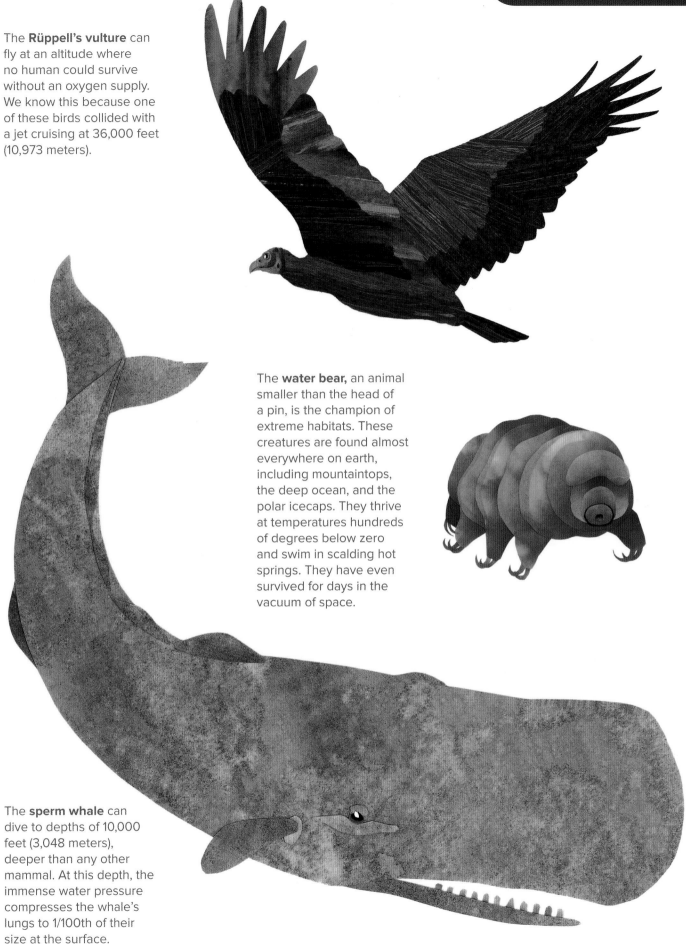

The **Rüppell's vulture** can fly at an altitude where no human could survive without an oxygen supply. We know this because one of these birds collided with a jet cruising at 36,000 feet (10,973 meters).

The **water bear,** an animal smaller than the head of a pin, is the champion of extreme habitats. These creatures are found almost everywhere on earth, including mountaintops, the deep ocean, and the polar icecaps. They thrive at temperatures hundreds of degrees below zero and swim in scalding hot springs. They have even survived for days in the vacuum of space.

The **sperm whale** can dive to depths of 10,000 feet (3,048 meters), deeper than any other mammal. At this depth, the immense water pressure compresses the whale's lungs to 1/100th of their size at the surface.

Deadliest to humans

The animals most dangerous to humans are not always the ones that people are most afraid of. Here are some dangerous creatures and the estimated number of human deaths they cause around the world each year.

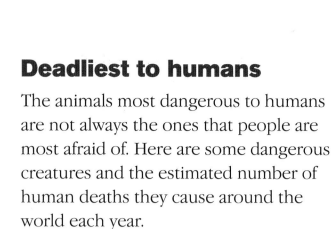

The great white shark is one of the most widely feared animals, but it probably kills only one or two people annually.

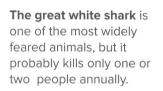

The **box jellyfish** is one of the most venomous animals in the world. It is responsible for about 60 deaths.

The **hippopotamus** defends its territory aggressively. A person who gets between a hippo and the water can be attacked. An estimated 100 people die this way.

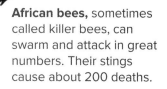

African bees, sometimes called killer bees, can swarm and attack in great numbers. Their stings cause about 200 deaths.

Most scorpions are not lethal. But the sting of the **fat-tailed scorpion** kills some 5,000 people.

Crocodiles kill as many as 1,000 people, mostly in Africa and Asia.

Dog attacks can be deadly. But in many parts of the world, the real danger is rabies, a disease caused most often by the bite of a dog. More than 50,000 perish from this disease.

An estimated 100,000 people die from snakebites each year. The **krait** is responsible for many of these deaths.

The world's most dangerous animal, by far, is the **mosquito**. Malaria and other diseases transmitted by the bite of this insect kill more than two million people every year.

145

Animal sizes compared

All of these animals are shown at the same scale.

Nile crocodile

rhinoceros

Andean condor

Galápagos tortoise

Quetzalcoatlus
extinct

emperor penguin

Siberian tiger

leatherback sea turtle

cheetah

camel

oarfish

gray wolf

great white shark

Velociraptor
extinct

Tyrannosaurus rex
extinct

bluefin tuna

blue whale

146

Komodo dragon

reticulated python

hippopotamus

Goliath frog

grizzly bear

gorilla

manatee

Argentinosaurus
extinct

colossal squid

giraffe

manta ray

African elephant

giant anteater

ostrich

flamingo

adult man

147

Life Spans: How Long Do Animals Live?

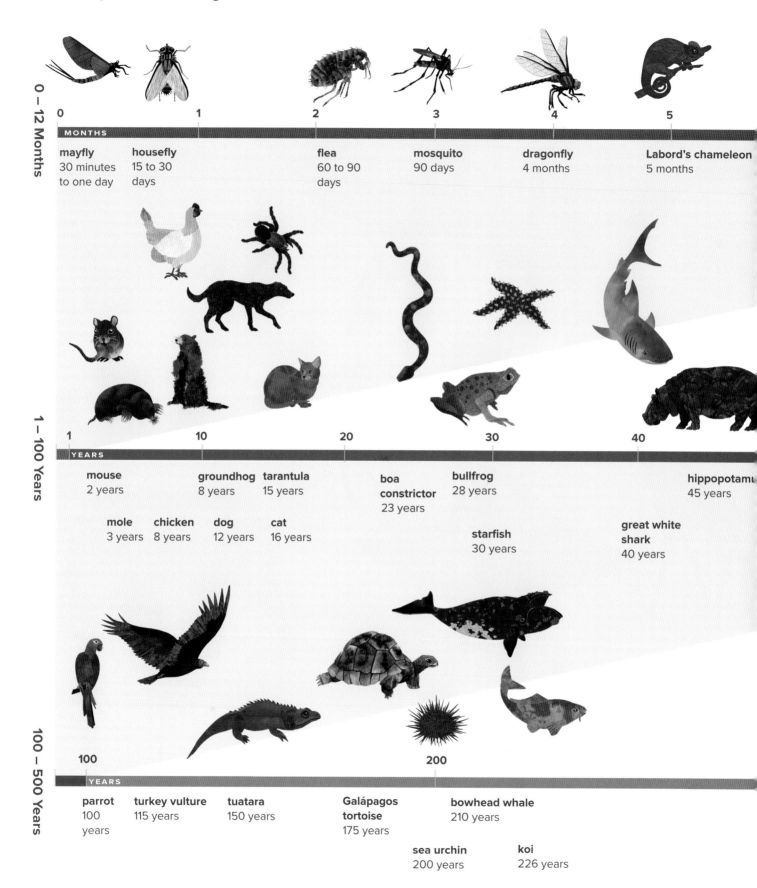

0 – 12 Months

0	1	2	3	4	5

MONTHS

mayfly
30 minutes
to one day

housefly
15 to 30
days

flea
60 to 90
days

mosquito
90 days

dragonfly
4 months

Labord's chameleon
5 months

1 – 100 Years

1	10	20	30	40

YEARS

mouse
2 years

groundhog
8 years

tarantula
15 years

**boa
constrictor**
23 years

bullfrog
28 years

hippopotamu
45 years

mole
3 years

chicken
8 years

dog
12 years

cat
16 years

starfish
30 years

**great white
shark**
40 years

100 – 500 Years

100	200

YEARS

parrot
100
years

turkey vulture
115 years

tuatara
150 years

**Galápagos
tortoise**
175 years

bowhead whale
210 years

sea urchin
200 years

koi
226 years

148

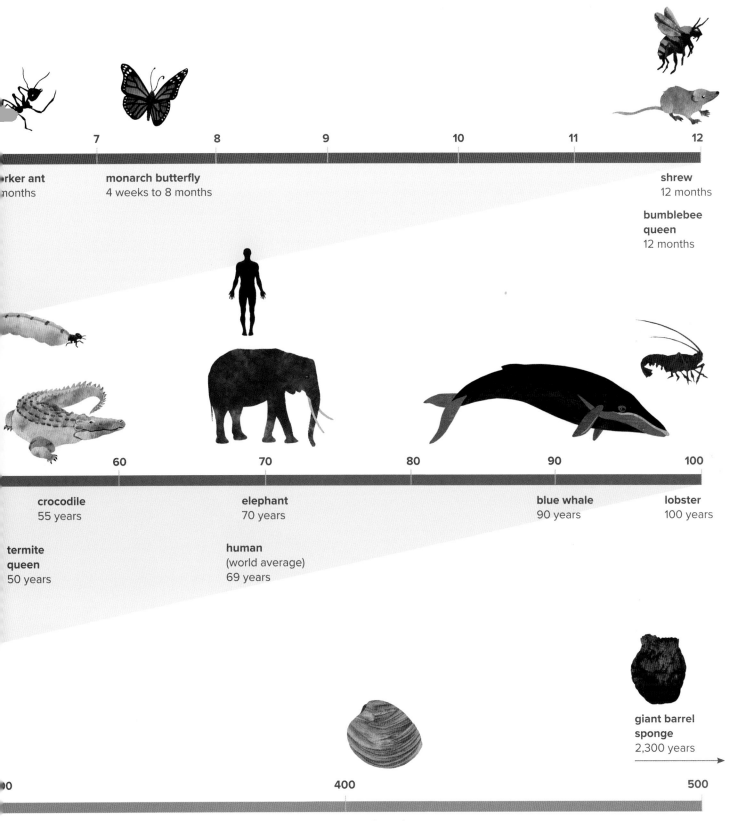

7 **8** **9** **10** **11** **12**

●rker ant
●nths

monarch butterfly
4 weeks to 8 months

shrew
12 months

**bumblebee
queen**
12 months

60 **70** **80** **90** **100**

crocodile
55 years

elephant
70 years

blue whale
90 years

lobster
100 years

**termite
queen**
50 years

human
(world average)
69 years

**giant barrel
sponge**
2,300 years →

●0 **400** **500**

quahog clam
410 years

The Story of Life

The story of life on earth is one of constant destruction, renewal, and change. Beginning with a single-celled organism that appeared more than 3½ billion years ago, life has taken on an astounding number of forms. Over and over, living things have grown more and more diverse, only to experience some catastrophe — severe climate change, massive volcanic eruptions, or the impact of a comet or asteroid — that killed off most of them. After each of these mass extinctions, millions of new organisms have gradually appeared, taking advantage of the gaps left behind.

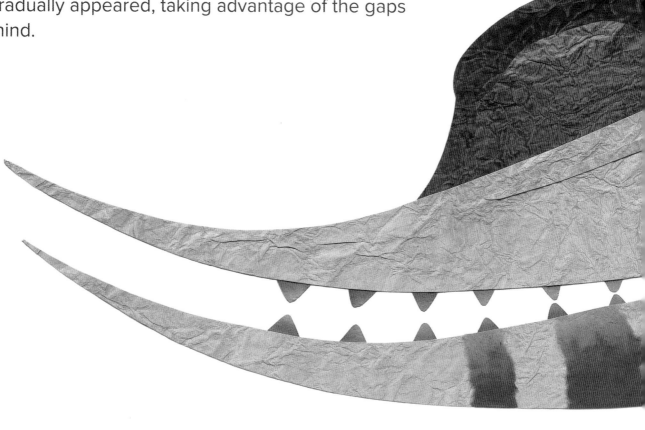

THE EARLY EARTH   THE FIRST LIFE   WE'RE ALL RELATED   A BRIEF HISTORY OF LIFE

Dsungaripterus (*jung-ah-rip-ter-us*) was a flying reptile the size of a condor, the largest flying bird alive today. It lived more than 100 million years ago.

THE THEORY OF EVOLUTION

SURVIVAL OF THE FITTEST

VARIATION AND MUTATION

GOOD DESIGNS

The early earth

The earth formed more than 4½ billion years ago from a disk of dust and debris circling the sun. For a long time the planet was a seething ball of molten rock. Its surface was bombarded by asteroids and comets, and its atmosphere was a soup of poisonous gasses.

The first life

After about 600 million years, the earth had cooled enough for oceans to form. A few hundred million years later, microscopic single-celled organisms were thriving in these early seas.

We don't know how or where life on earth got its start. It might have appeared in a shallow tidal pool, in a volcanic hot spring, or deep underground. Some scientists think that life might even have hitchhiked to earth on a comet or asteroid.

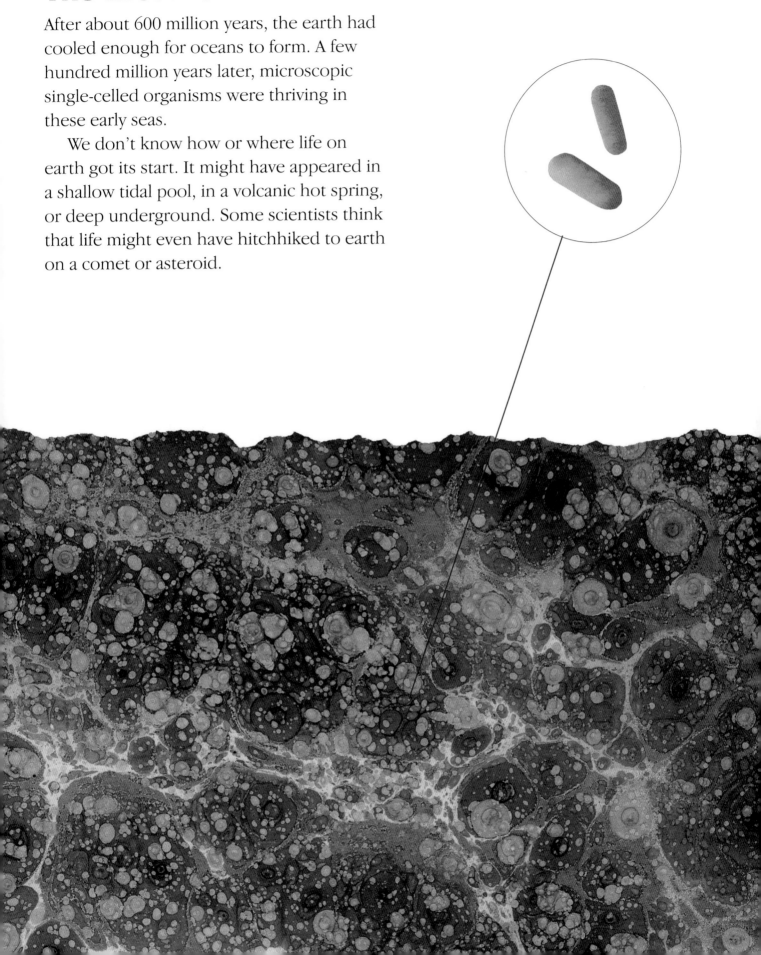

We're all related.

All life on earth — past and present — is descended from a microscopic single-celled organism, similar to modern bacteria, that lived more than 3½ billion years ago.

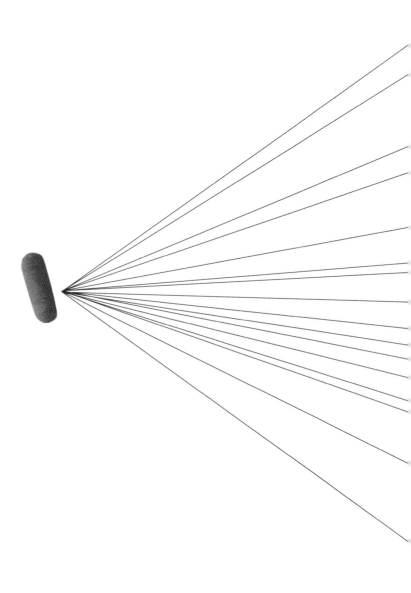

This ancient single-celled organism is shown enlarged about 20,000 times. One hundred of these cells lined up side by side would match the thickness of a human hair.

A brief history of life

1¼ billion years ago

The first multicellular lifeforms — primitive algae — appear in the ocean.

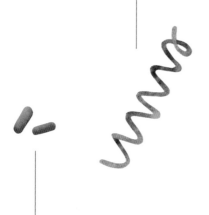

3½ billion years ago

The first single-celled organisms appear.

650 million years ago

The first animals — comb jellies, jellyfishes, and sponges — are living in the seas.

580 million years ago

More complex animals
have appeared. Many look
like plants and spend their
lives anchored to the sea
floor.

510 million years ago

Nautiloids, the ancestors
of modern-day squids and
octopuses, are the top
predators. Some of these
large, free-swimming
animals are as long as an
automobile.

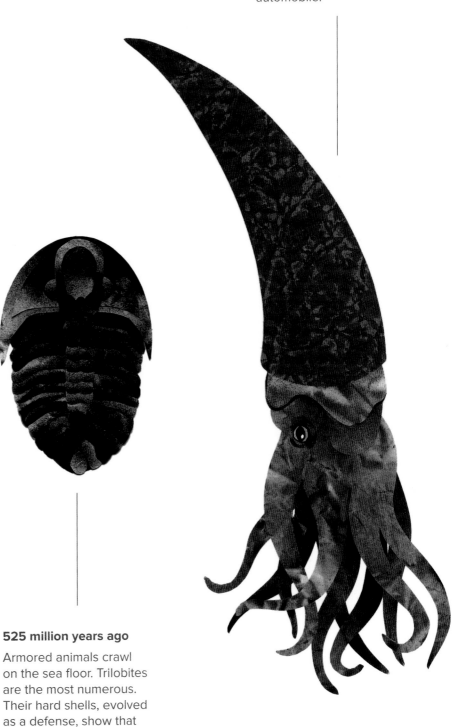

525 million years ago

Armored animals crawl
on the sea floor. Trilobites
are the most numerous.
Their hard shells, evolved
as a defense, show that
predators are now hunting
and eating other creatures.

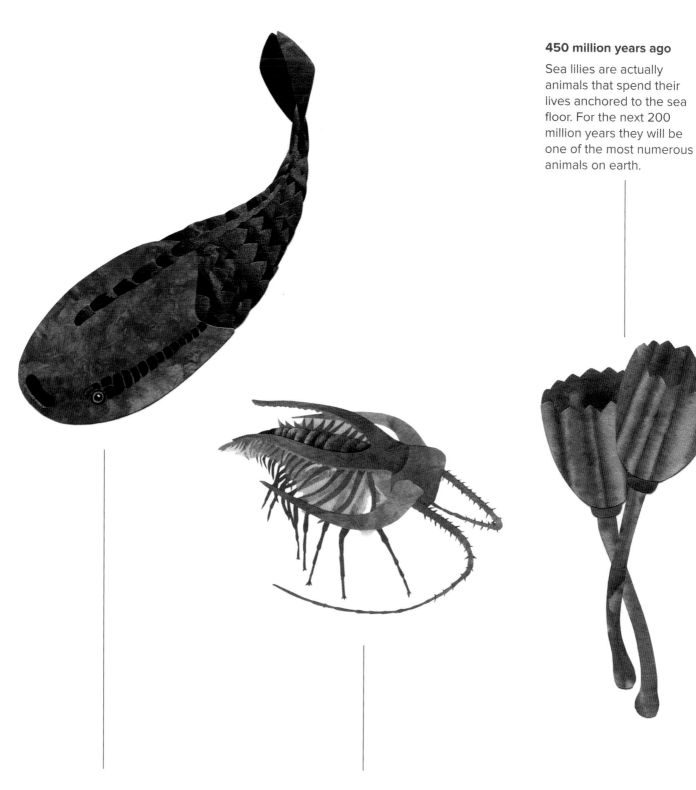

450 million years ago

Sea lilies are actually animals that spend their lives anchored to the sea floor. For the next 200 million years they will be one of the most numerous animals on earth.

510 million years ago

Primitive armored fish swim in the seas.

505 million years ago

Strange segmented animals, unlike any alive today, prowl the oceans. The creature above could fit in a teaspoon, but the largest of these animals was the size of a grown man.

425 million years ago

The sea is a dangerous place, full of frightening predators and fierce competition for food. Taking advantage of a new habitat, scorpions and millipedes crawl from the water and begin to make their way on land.

340 million years ago

Amphibians evolve from four-legged fish. They will be the dominant land animals for the next 100 million years. The largest of them is the length of a school bus.

430 million years ago

Mosses move to the land. Some primitive algae and molds left the water millions of years before, but up until now, all complex life — plants and animals — has been found only in the oceans.

400 million years ago

A four-legged fish pulls itself from the water and becomes the first vertebrate to live on dry land.

310 million years ago

The first reptiles, small animals that resemble modern-day lizards, make their appearance.

325 million years ago

Earth's climate is warm, and towering club mosses 130 feet (40 meters) tall form forests that cover much of the land.

300 million years ago

Winged insects, the first flying animals, have been living on the land for 50 million years. By now, some of them have become huge. There are dragonflies with a 2½ foot (76 centimeters) wingspan.

275 million years ago

One group of reptiles evolves into the therapsids, ancestors of the mammals.

225 million years ago

The first dinosaurs — chicken-size animals that run on two legs — are here. In the future, dinosaurs will become much larger. They will be the dominant land animals for the next 160 million years.

150 million years ago

Some small flying or gliding animals descended from dinosaurs take to the air. They are sometimes considered the first birds.

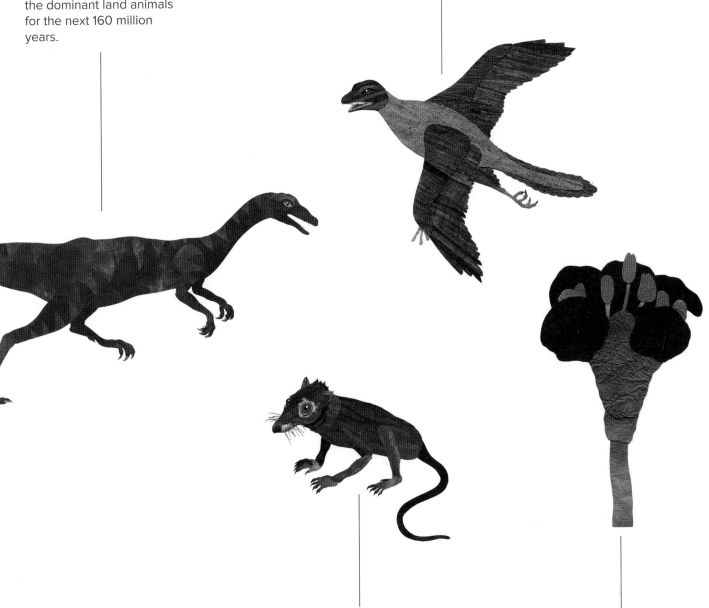

220 million years ago

The first mammals are small, shrewlike animals. Most sleep during the day and are active at night to avoid the larger, fiercer dinosaurs.

140 million years ago

The first flowering plants appear.

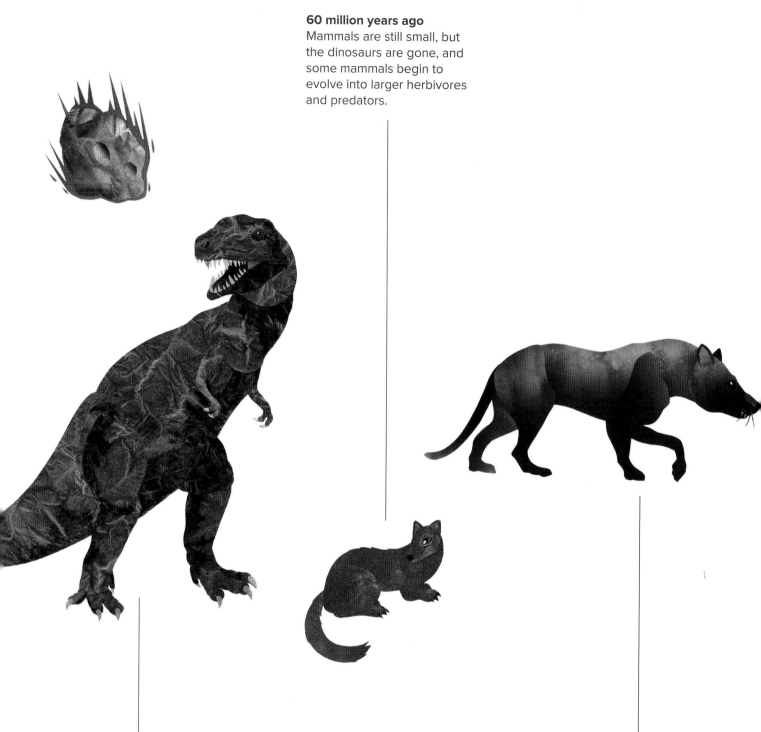

60 million years ago
Mammals are still small, but the dinosaurs are gone, and some mammals begin to evolve into larger herbivores and predators.

65 million years ago
The end of *Tyrannosaurus rex* and the rest of the dinosaurs. Asteroid impact and massive volcanic eruptions probably seal their fate.

40 million years ago
A predatory mammal — an ancestor of the hyena — is the size of a rhinoceros.

15 million years ago
The ten-foot (3-meter)-tall terror bird is one of the dominant predators on land.

3½ million years ago
The earliest upright human ancestors take their first steps.

5 million years ago
The 20-foot (6-meter)-tall giant ground sloth and other huge plant-eating mammals roam the world's grasslands.

200,000 years ago
Modern humans — people that look like us — appear in Africa.

The theory of evolution

As recently as two hundred years ago, most people believed that all plants and animals were created at the same time in the not-too-distant past. New discoveries, however, were beginning to challenge this belief. Perhaps, some scientists thought, modern plants and animals were descended from common ancestors and had changed over time.

Explorers were returning from distant places with strange creatures, such as this **tarsier**, that most people had never seen before. Scientists realized that many of these animals were related to more familiar species.

Geologists were also beginning to realize that the earth was much older than anyone had imagined. This was important — it meant that life had had a long time to develop.

All over the world, new fossils — the preserved remains of ancient life — were being unearthed. Many of these fossils were clearly the remains of animals no longer alive. It began to seem likely that life had not always remained the same.

In 1831 the naturalist Charles Darwin left England to sail around the world on a scientific expedition. During his voyage, he visited the Galápagos, an isolated group of islands in the Pacific Ocean. There he found a population of finches that were to give him important clues about the way evolution works. Darwin believed that all the finches were the descendants of the same two birds — perhaps a pair that had been blown to the islands in a storm. He noticed, however, that the birds' beaks were shaped differently on each island. Darwin believed that small changes over many generations had resulted in fourteen different species of finch, each with a beak best suited to the kind of food available on its island.

The theory that Darwin proposed to explain these observations — the theory of evolution — has been called "the most important idea anyone ever had."

Darwin spent five years on HMS *Beagle,* collecting plants and animals from many parts of the world.

In 1859, Darwin published *On the Origin of Species,* the book that explained how the theory of evolution works.

The Galápagos finches helped Darwin formulate his theory.

This finch has a short, strong beak for cracking hard seeds.

This one has a beak that's shaped to hold a twig. The bird uses it to pry insects from tree bark.

This bird has a curved beak ideal for eating plants and soft fruit.

This finch uses its long beak to catch insects.

Survival of the fittest

Darwin knew that most plants and animals produce far more offspring than can survive. Many fish, amphibians, and insects lay hundreds, thousands, or millions of eggs. If all of the descendants of even a single pair of these animals survived, they would soon overrun the earth. Most of the young, however, perish before they can grow up and reproduce. The slower, weaker, and less hardy animals are more likely to die or be killed. The offspring best at escaping predators, finding food, and surviving hardships are the ones most likely to survive and have babies. Darwin called this process natural selection, or survival of the fittest.

Natural selection at work

A mother frog lays 3,000 eggs. Most of these eggs are eaten before they can hatch.

Two hundred tadpoles hatch, but most are eaten by predators. Only eight survive to become frogs. And life is not easy for the young amphibians . . .

One frog can't catch enough insects to eat. It starves.

This frog is swallowed by a snake.

This young frog has good eyesight. It is better able to avoid predators and spot insects to eat. It survives.

One frog dies after moving to a pond that dries up.

This frog is speared by a bird.

A fish swallows this frog.

One lucky frog can jump a little farther than its brothers and sisters. It escapes its predators and survives.

This frog is devoured by a toad.

Of the eight frogs, only two survive. One has sharp eyesight and the other is a good leaper. If these frogs reproduce, they may pass on these advantages on to their offspring, who will also be more likely to survive.

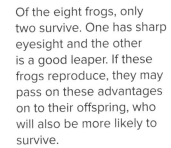

Variation and mutation

It's easy to see that creatures poorly suited to their environment are less likely to survive. What makes some animals more fit — more likely to survive?

Scientists in Darwin's time didn't understand how traits were passed from a mother and father to the next generation. We know now that offspring can differ from their parents through either variation or mutation. Some of these differences are harmful, and the animals that acquire them probably won't live long enough to reproduce. Sometimes, however, a variation or mutation gives an animal an advantage that helps it survive.

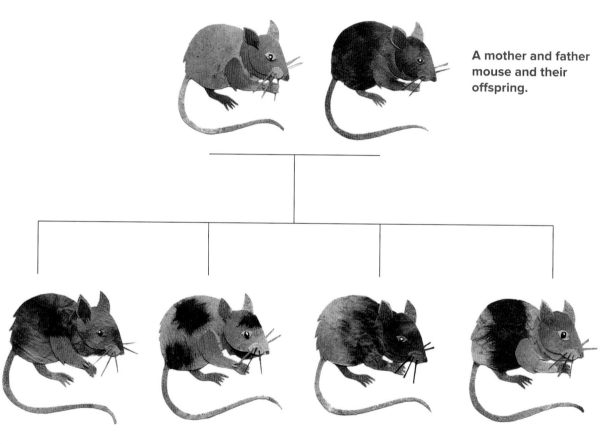

A mother and father mouse and their offspring.

Variation

When animals reproduce most have babies that combine the qualities of the mother and the father. Since each combination is a little different, there are natural variations among offspring. Some will be taller, some shorter; some darker, some lighter; some faster, and some slower.

Some of these variations help an animal survive. A faster mouse, for instance, will be more likely to escape predators and grow up to have babies of its own.

Mutation

Every so often, something unusual happens when animals reproduce. Mutations — completely new features — appear in the next generation. Mutations are random, and most are harmful, making an animal less likely to survive. But sometimes a new feature provides an advantage. When that happens, the mutation is likely to be passed on.

A mother and father fish and their offspring.

A harmful mutation

This fish is an albino — a mutation has resulted in it being completely white. A white fish is much easier for a predator to spot, so this fish probably won't survive long enough to reproduce.

No mutations

This fish looks a lot like its parents.

A helpful mutation

This fish was born with mottled skin that makes it difficult to spot on a pebbly stream bottom. It is likely to survive and may pass on this new coloration to some of its offspring.

Good designs

Some animals are so well suited for survival that they haven't changed much in a long time. For these creatures, no variation or mutation is likely to offer much of an advantage.

Fossil **cockroaches** 350 million years old have been unearthed.

The earliest **turtles** lived more than 200 million years ago.

The first **crocodiles** appeared 100 million years ago.

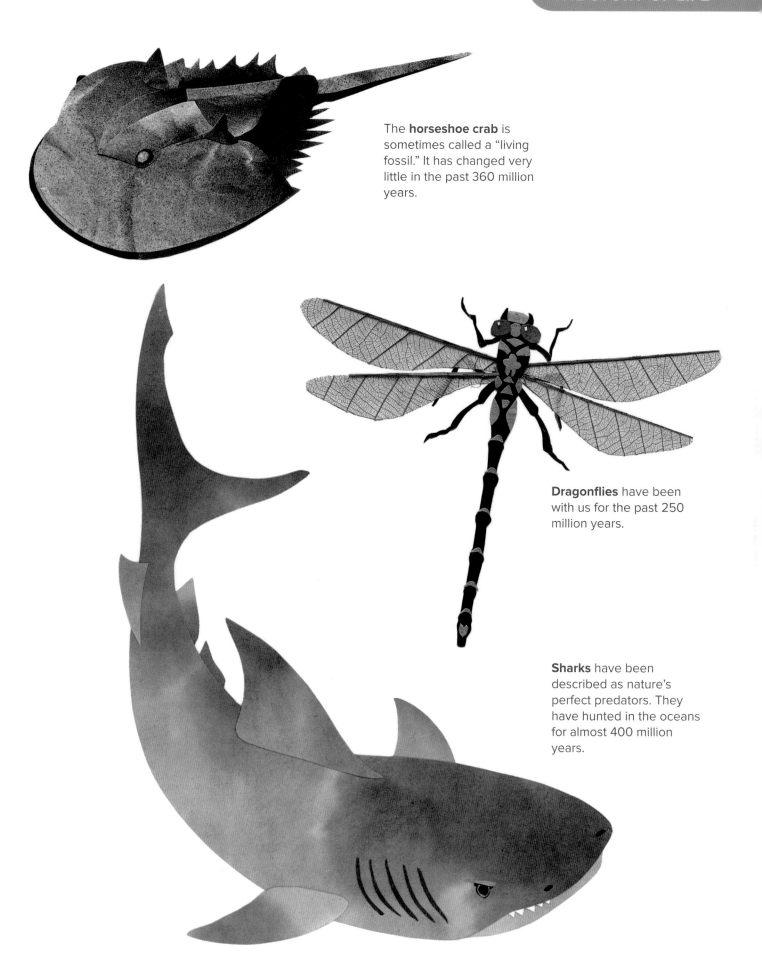

The **horseshoe crab** is sometimes called a "living fossil." It has changed very little in the past 360 million years.

Dragonflies have been with us for the past 250 million years.

Sharks have been described as nature's perfect predators. They have hunted in the oceans for almost 400 million years.

A timeline of animal life

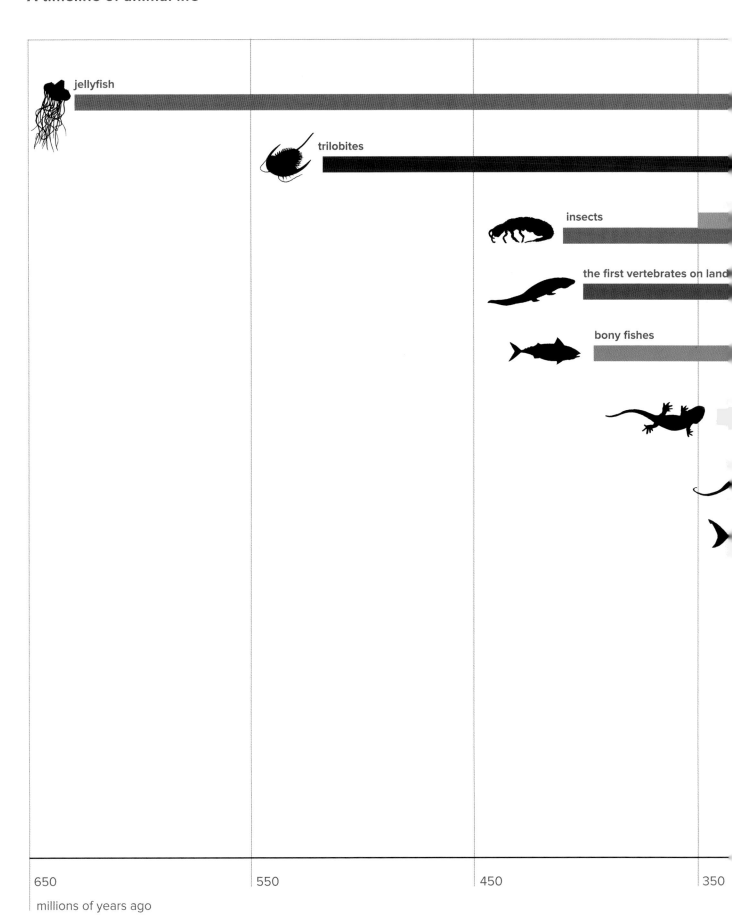

jellyfish

trilobites

insects

the first vertebrates on land

bony fishes

650   550   450   350

millions of years ago

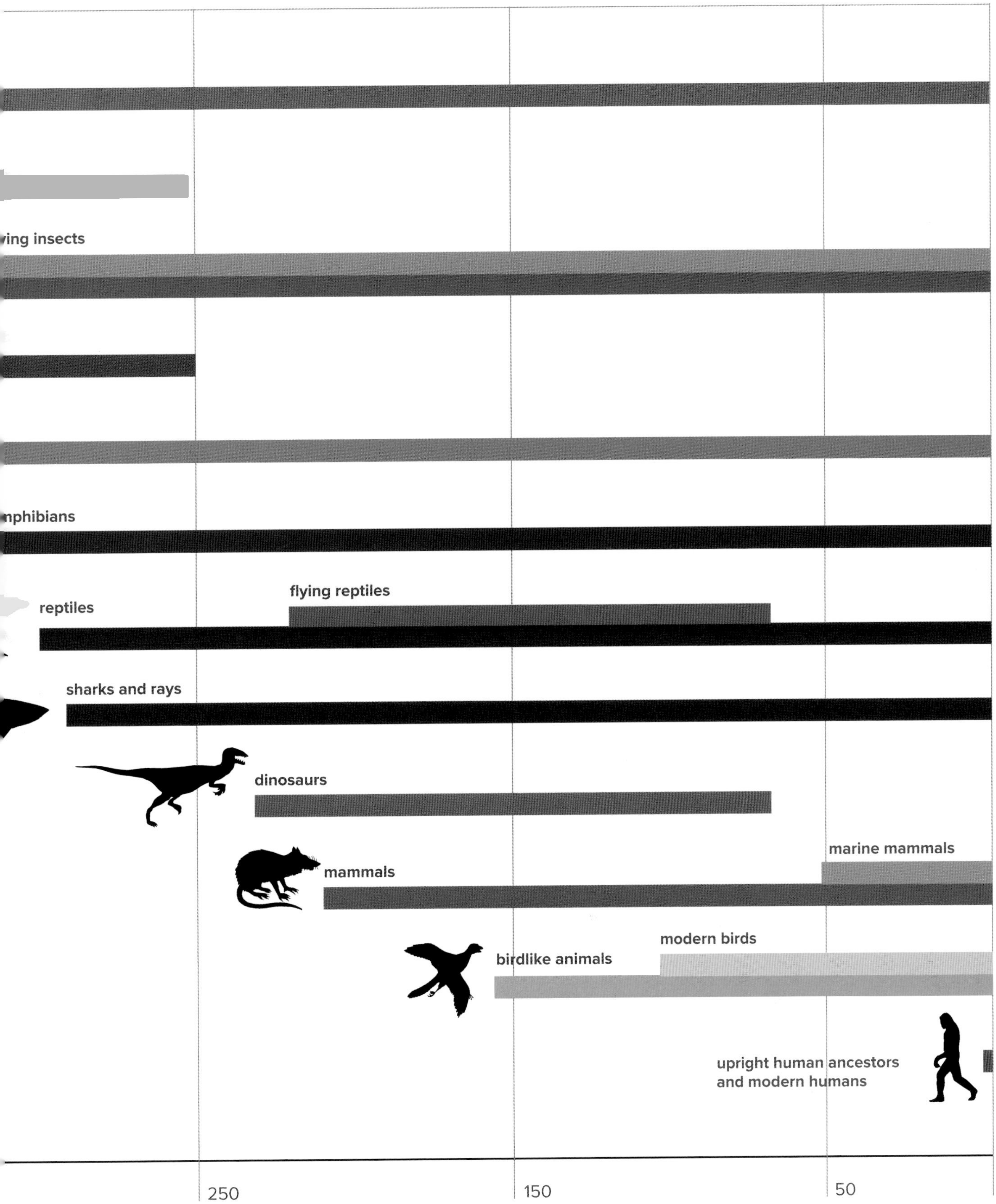

ing insects

mphibians

reptiles

flying reptiles

sharks and rays

dinosaurs

marine mammals

mammals

modern birds

birdlike animals

upright human ancestors
and modern humans

250

150

50

A history of the earth in 24 hours

It's not easy to get a sense of how old the earth really is. This timeline shows our planet's 4½ billion-year history compressed into a single twenty-four-hour day.

(00:00)
The earth forms.

12:00 a.m. 1:00 a.m. 2:00 a.m. 3:00 a.m. 4:00 a.m. 5:00 a.m. 6:00 a.m. 7:00 a.m. 8:00 a.m. 9:00 a.m. 10:00 a.m. 11:00 a.m. 12:00

5:00 a.m.
The first life appears.

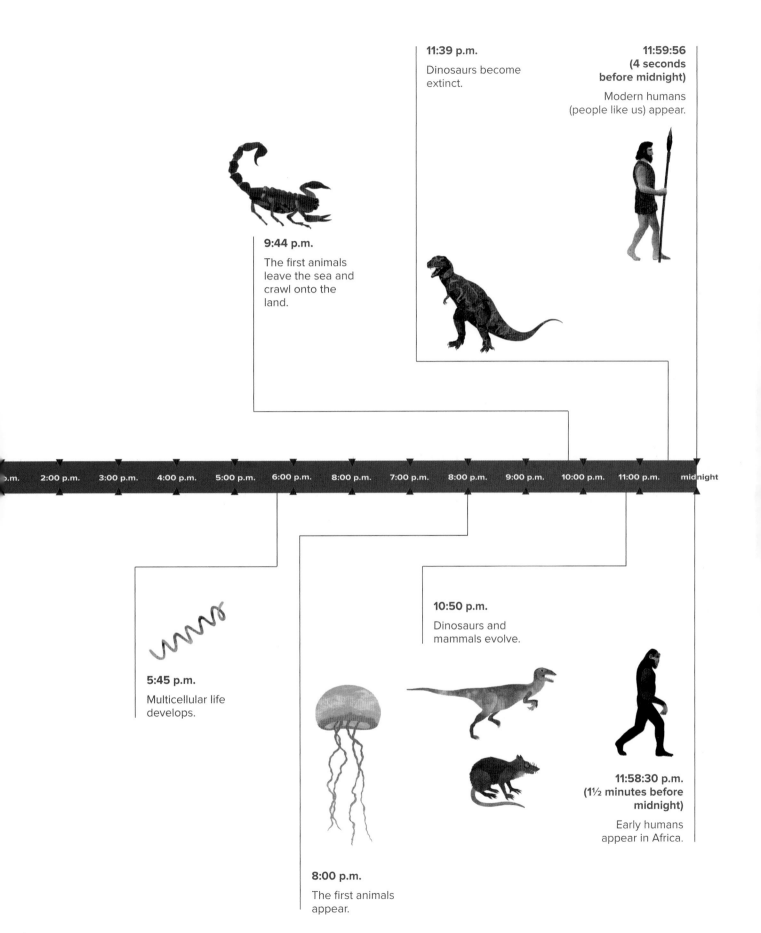

11:39 p.m.
Dinosaurs become extinct.

11:59:56 (4 seconds before midnight)
Modern humans (people like us) appear.

9:44 p.m.
The first animals leave the sea and crawl onto the land.

5:45 p.m.
Multicellular life develops.

10:50 p.m.
Dinosaurs and mammals evolve.

11:58:30 p.m. (1½ minutes before midnight)
Early humans appear in Africa.

8:00 p.m.
The first animals appear.

2:00 p.m. 3:00 p.m. 4:00 p.m. 5:00 p.m. 6:00 p.m. 8:00 p.m. 7:00 p.m. 8:00 p.m. 9:00 p.m. 10:00 p.m. 11:00 p.m. midnight

More Animal Facts

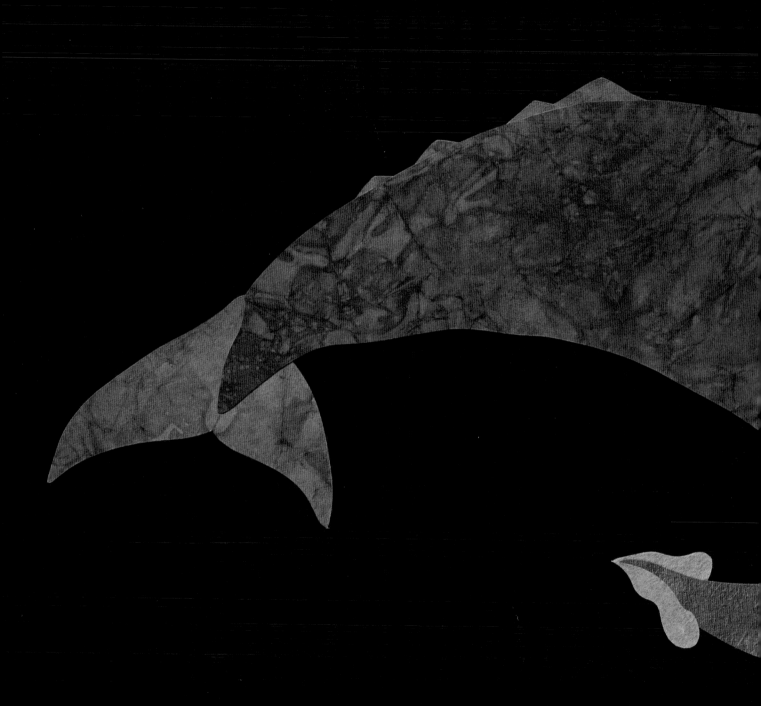

Sperm whale and colossal squid

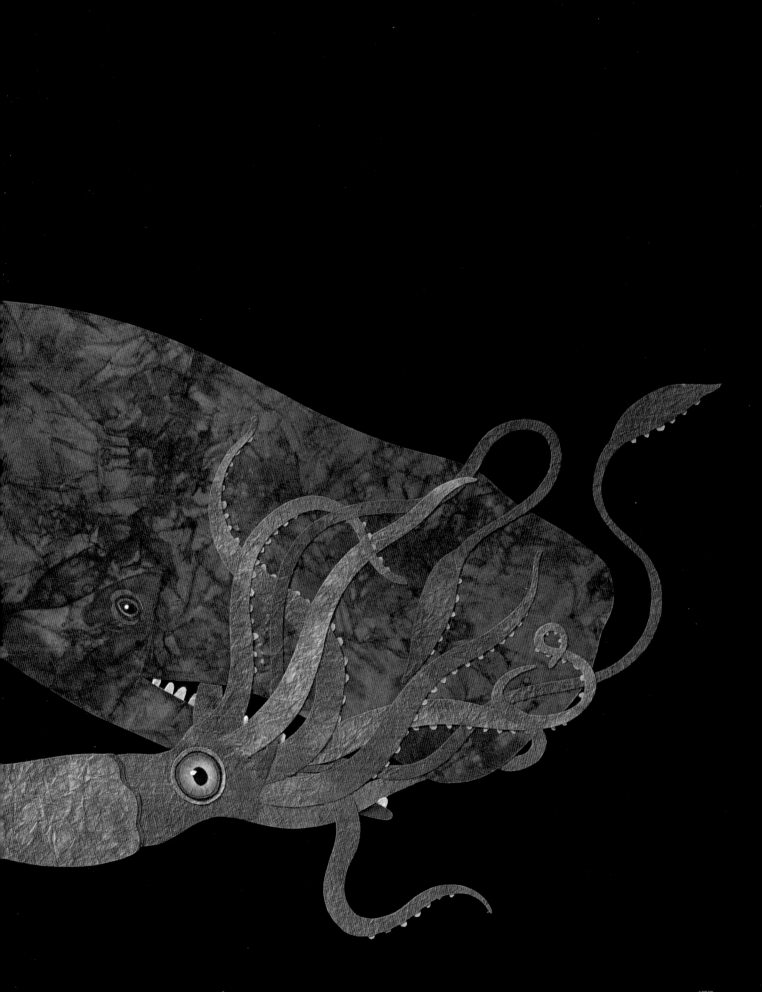

Here you will find more information about many of the animals in this book. After each animal's name is the page number, or numbers, where that animal appears.

African bee (*144*)
Length: ¾ inch (2 centimeters)
Habitat: South and Central America, the southern and southwestern United States
Diet: flower pollen and nectar
Fact: These bees are no more venomous than honeybees, but they are more aggressive and quick to attack.

African elephant (*49, 57, 113, 147*)
Height: 11 feet (3½ meters)
Weight: 13,000 pounds (5,900 kilograms)
Habitat: grasslands and forests in central and southern Africa
Diet: grass, shrubs, leaves, and bark
Fact: An elephant can eat 600 pounds (272 kilograms) of food a day.

African foam grasshopper (*98*)
Length: 3 inches (7½ centimeters)
Habitat: scrublands of South Africa
Diet: milkweed
Fact: The poison in the grasshopper's foam comes from the toxins in the milkweed plants it feeds on.

alligator (*5, 43*)
Length: 13 feet (4 meters)
Weight: 800 pounds (363 kilograms)
Habitat: rivers, lakes, and swamps of the southeastern United States
Diet: fish, turtles, snakes, and small mammals
Fact: Alligators will also eat dogs, cats, and, in rare instances, humans.

alligator snapping turtle (*78*)
Weight: 200 pounds (91 kilograms)
Habitat: canals, rivers, lakes, and swamps of the southeastern United States
Diet: fish, frogs, other turtles, and dead animals
Fact: A snapping turtle can hold its breath for as long as fifty minutes.

Amau frog (*133*)
Length: ³/₁₀ inch (7½ millimeters)
Habitat: tropical forests in

Papua New Guinea
Diet: small invertebrates
Fact: This frog was discovered by scientists in 2009 and officially named the world's smallest vertebrate in 2012.

archerfish (*82*)
Length: 10 inches (25 centimeters)
Habitat: fresh and salt water on the coasts of Australia and the east coast of Africa
Diet: flies, beetles, or other insects
Fact: Archer fish can shoot down insects from as far as 6½ feet (2 meters) away.

arctic hare (*30*)
Length: 2 feet (61 centimeters)
Habitat: northern Canada
Diet: berries, leaves, roots, and mosses
Fact: The arctic hare's coat changes from brown to white in winter.

Argentinosaurus (*113*)
Length: 108 feet (33 meters)
Habitat: South America (95 million years ago)
Diet: evergreen trees and shrubs
Fact: It probably took 40 years for this dinosaur to reach its full size.

armadillo lizard (*96*)
Length: 10 inches (25 centimeters)
Habitat: dry, rocky land along the west coast of South Africa
Diet: insects and spiders
Fact: Mother armadillo lizards give birth to live babies.

Asian koel (*47*)
Length: 18 inches (46 centimeters)
Habitat: woodlands of southern Asia
Diet: insects and small animals
Fact: The koel's diet includes some kinds of fruit that are poisonous to mammals.

assassin bug (*81*)
Length: one inch (2½ centimeters)
Habitat: worldwide
Diet: other insects
Fact: Assassin bugs are also known as "kissing bugs" because they sometimes bite sleeping humans on the lips or eyelids, causing painful swelling.

Atlas moth (*130*)
Wingspan: 12 inches (30 centimeters)
Habitat: Southeast Asia
Diet: flower nectar
Fact: This moth gets its name from

either the map-like patterns on its wings, or from Atlas, an gigantic god in Greek mythology.

Barbados thread snake (*133*)
Length: 4 inches (10 centimeters)
Habitat: the Caribbean island of Barbados
Diet: termites, ants, and insect larvae
Fact: Scientists believe that this is probably as small as a snake can get — any smaller and it won't be able to find suitable prey.

bee hummingbird (*132*)
Length: 2 inches (5 centimeters)
Weight: ¹/₂₀ ounce (1½ grams)
Habitat: Cuba
Diet: nectar, and small insects
Fact: This bird can eat half its weight in food every day.

Bengal tiger (*73*)
Length (nose to tail): 10 feet (3 meters)
Weight: 500 pounds (227 kilograms)
Habitat: grasslands and forests of South Asia
Diet: buffalo, deer, wild pigs, and other mammals; occasionally humans
Fact: There are only about 2,500 of these big cats left in the wild.

blackchin tilapia (*40*)
Length: 10 inches (25 centimeters)
Habitat: brackish streams and lagoons in tropical Africa
Diet: algae, microorganisms, and dead plants and animals
Fact: This fish is now common in Florida, where it was released from aquariums into the wild in the 1950s.

black bear (*5*)
Weight: up to 600 pounds (272 kilograms)
Habitat: mountains and forests in the United States and Canada
Diet: seeds, berries, insects, fish, large and small mammals
Fact: Black bears hibernate — they sleep through the winter without eating.

black rat (*61*)
Length (head and body): 9 inches (23 centimeters)
Habitat: worldwide, wherever humans live
Diet: seeds, fruit, leaves, fungi, small animals, and garbage
Fact: Fleas carried by these rats spread

the bubonic plague, a disease that killed one-third of the world's human population in the fourteenth century.

 black swallower (*73*)
Length: 10 inches (25 centimeters)
Habitat: Atlantic Ocean
Diet: other fish
Fact: Sometimes these fish swallow prey that is too large to digest — a fatal mistake.

 black widow spider (*31, 46*)
Size (including legs): 1½ inches (4 centimeters) across
Habitat: beneath rocks and under buildings in warm parts of the world
Diet: insects and other spiders
Fact: Unlike the webs of many spiders, the black widow's web is messy and disorganized.

 blind shrimp (*106*)
Length: 2 inches (5 centimeters)
Habitat: coral reefs in the southern Pacific Ocean
Diet: plankton, dead animals
Fact: This shrimp keeps one antenna in contact with a goby, a small fish it shares a burrow with. The goby will warn the shrimp of approaching danger by wagging its tail.

 blue bird of paradise (*26*)
Length: 12 inches (30 centimeters)
Habitat: mountain forests of New Guinea
Diet: fruit and insects
Fact: In the past, birds of paradise were hunted almost to extinction for their feathers, which were used to decorate women's hats.

 blue-footed booby (*30*)
Wingspan: 5 feet (1½ meters)
Habitat: The western coasts of Central and South America; the Galápagos Islands
Diet: small fish
Fact: These birds are excellent divers and swimmers.

 blue heron (*72, 84*)
Height: four feet (1¼ meters)
Habitat: ponds, rivers, bays, and marshes in North America
Diet: fish, snakes, frogs, and rodents
Fact: Blue herons nest in colonies that include as many as 500 birds.

 blue-ringed octopus (*80*)
Size (including legs): 8 inches (20 centimeters) across
Habitat: tide pools and reefs in the western Pacific Ocean
Diet: crabs and small fish
Fact: A person bitten by this highly venomous octopus can die within an hour.

 blue-tailed skink (*103*)
Length: 10 inches (25 centimeters)
Habitat: warm regions throughout the world
Diet: insects and spiders
Fact: Blue-tailed skinks are good at climbing trees and are often found high above the ground.

 blue whale (*39, 112, 139, 146, 149*)
Length: 110 feet (34 meters)
Habitat: oceans worldwide
Diet: krill (shrimplike animals)
Fact: A blue whale eats more than 7,500 pounds (3,400 kilograms) of krill a day.

 blue-winged grasshopper (*102*)
Length: 1 inch (2½ centimeters)
Habitat: dry regions of Europe, northern Africa, and North America
Diet: leaves and grass
Fact: These grasshoppers are well camouflaged and difficult to spot until they open their wings.

 bolas spider (*83*)
Length: ½ inch (13 millimeters)
Habitat: the Americas, Africa, Australia, and Asia
Diet: moths and other insects
Fact: A chemical lure produced by this spider imitates the odor of a female moth, luring male moths to their death.

 bombardier beetle (*98*)
Length: ¾ inch (2 centimeters)
Habitat: wooded and grassy areas in North America, South America, Europe, Africa, and Australia
Diet: other insects
Fact: This beetle fires its hot chemical spray at a rate of 500 bursts a second.

 bootlace worm (*136*)
Length: up to 180 feet (55 meters)
Habitat: sea floors along the coast of Europe
Diet: crustaceans and other worms
Fact: It's difficult to know exactly

how long these worms are, because their bodies stretch as they are being measured.

 bowhead whale (*140, 148*)
Length: 40 feet (12 meters)
Habitat: Arctic Ocean and nearby seas
Diet: krill, other invertebrates, and fish
Fact: These whales use their huge heads to break through thick sea ice.

 box jellyfish (*80*)
Length: 10 feet (3 meters)
Habitat: coastal waters of northern Australia and the Indo-Pacific Ocean
Diet: small fish, shrimp, and jellyfish
Fact: This jellyfish has 24 eyes arranged around its bell. It spots its prey and actively pursues it.

 boxer crab (*95*)
Width: ½ inch (13 millimeters)
Habitat: Indian and Pacific Oceans
Diet: plants, dead animals, and zooplankton
Fact: If it can't find an anemone, the boxer crab will try to fool an attacker by holding up a piece of sponge or coral.

 brown bear (*13*)
Height (standing): 13 feet (4 meters)
Weight: 1,400 pounds (635 kilograms)
Habitat: mountainous and arctic regions of the northern United States, Canada, Europe, and Asia
Diet: seeds, berries, insects, fish, and large and small mammals
Fact: The brown bear (along with its cousin the polar bear) is the largest predator living on land.

 Budgett's frog (*102*)
Length: 5 inches (12½ centimeters)
Habitat: rivers, streams, and lakes in southern South America
Diet: insects and small aquatic animals
Fact: This frog has two fanglike protrusions in its mouth. If cornered, it will bite.

 bumblebee (*61, 149*)
Length: ¾ inch (19 millimeters)
Habitat: temperate regions worldwide
Diet: nectar and pollen
Fact: In cold weather, bumblebees can raise their body temperature by rapidly vibrating their flight muscles.

bumblebee bat (*132*)
Length: 1¼ inches
(3 centimeters)
Habitat: caves and forests in
Southeast Asia
Diet: small insects and spiders
Fact: Scientists first learned of this bat,
the world's smallest, in 1974.

burrowing owl (*92*)
Height: 10 inches
(25 centimeters)
Habitat: grasslands and
deserts in western North America, the
Caribbean, and South America
Diet: insects, mice, and small animals
Fact: Burrowing owls often move into
underground homes excavated by
prairie dogs or other burrowing animals.

burying beetle (*32*)
Length: 1¼ inches
(3 centimeters)
Habitat: central
United States
Diet: dead animals
Fact: This beetle can detect an animal's
carcass within an hour of its death.

cane toad (*94*)
Length: 6 inches
(15 centimeters)
Habitat: southern United
States, Central and South America, and
Australia
Diet: carrion, garbage, and insects
Fact: A few thousand cane toads were
released in Australia in the 1930s to eat
insect pests. They now number in the
millions and have become a serious
problem, since native animals that try to
eat them are poisoned.

Cape buffalo (*104*)
Weight: 2,000 pounds
(900 kilograms)
Habitat: woodlands and
plains of central and southern Africa
Diet: grass and leaves
Fact: This buffalo has been known to
attack and kill a full-grown lion.

Cape stag beetle (*28*)
Size: 1 inch (2½ centimeters)
Habitat: mountains of
South Africa
Diet: wood and decaying wood
Fact: These beetles are threatened
by insect collectors, who will pay
thousands of dollars for a single
specimen.

cassowary (*105*)
Height: 6½ feet (2 meters)
Habitat: forests of
New Guinea and
northeastern Australia

Diet: fruit, insects, frogs, and snakes
Fact: The cassowary's bony "helmet"
makes it the only armored bird.

cecropia (*26*)
Wingspan: 6 inches
(15 centimeters)
Habitat: eastern United
States and Canada
Diet: leaves of trees and shrubs
Fact: Only the cecropia larva — the
caterpillar — eats. The adult moth does
not. Its only purpose is to mate.

cedar beetle (*17*)
Length: ½ inch
(13 millimeters)
Habitat: North America
Diet: cedar trees
Fact: In their larval stage, these beetles
are predators, feeding on cicada larvae.

channel catfish (*59*)
Weight: up to 58 pounds
(26 kilograms)
Habitat: Canada, the eastern
United States, and northern Mexico
Diet: insects, worms, clams, and fish
Fact: Unlike most fish, channel catfish
have no scales — their skin is smooth.

cheetah (*71, 148*)
Length: 4½ feet
(137 centimeters)
Habitat: African plains
Diet: rabbits, antelopes, and other small
animals
Fact: Cheetahs can run at top speed
for only a few seconds. If they don't
catch their prey quickly, it will probably
escape.

Chilean rose tarantula (*105*)
Size (including legs):
5 inches (12½ centimeters)
Habitat: desert regions of
South America
Diet: grasshoppers, moths, beetles,
roaches and other invertebrates
Fact: The Chilean rose tarantula is the
most popular species of pet tarantula.

cicada (*139*)
Length: 2 inches
(5 centimeters)
Habitat: temperate regions
throughout the world
Diet: juice from the roots of trees
Fact: Cicada larvae live underground
for as long as 17 years. Millions of adults
emerge at the same time, overwhelming
predators with their numbers.

clownfish (*107*)
Length: 6 inches
(15 centimeters)
Habitat: coral reefs in the

southern Pacific Ocean
Diet: algae, plankton
Fact: Clownfish keep their host
anemone clean.

cockroach (*170*)
(American cockroach)
Length: 1½ inches
(4 centimeters)
Habitat: tropical regions of the world
Diet: decaying plants and animals, food
scraps and garbage
Fact: The American cockroach is also
known as a palmetto bug. It is the
largest of the 4,500 known species of
cockroach.

colossal squid (*54, 147, 177*)
Length: 46 feet (14 meters)
Habitat: southern Atlantic
and Pacific Oceans
Diet: fish and squid
Fact: This animal has never been
observed in the wild. We've only been
able to study dead colossal squid that
have become trapped in fishing nets or
washed up on the shore.

comb jelly (*24, 156*)
Size: ¼ inch (6 millimeters)
to 5 feet (1½ meters)
Habitat: oceans worldwide
Diet: animal plankton, other jellies
Fact: Many deep-sea comb jellies light
up, flashing like a neon sign. Their
bioluminescence probably helps them
by startling predators.

common frog (*53*)
Length: 3 inches
(7½ centimeters)
Habitat: throughout Europe
Diet: insects, snails, slugs, and worms
Fact: Common frogs can lighten or
darken their skin to blend in with their
surroundings.

corn snake (*61*)
Length: up to 6 feet
(1¾ meters)
Habitat: southeastern
United States
Diet: mice, rats, birds, and bats
Fact: Corn snakes are constrictors —
they squeeze their prey to death, then
swallow it whole.

crab spider (*75*)
Length: ⅜ inch
(1 centimeter)
Habitat: yellow or white
flowers throughout North America
Diet: bees, wasps, moths, and butterflies
Fact: Crab spiders get their name from
their scuttling sideways movement.

cricket (*57*)
Length: ¾ inch
(2 centimeters)
Habitat: throughout warm
regions of the world
Diet: decaying plant material and fungi
Fact: Count the number of cricket chirps
in 15 seconds and add 40 to get a
fairly accurate temperature reading (in
degrees Fahrenheit).

crocodile (Nile crocodile)
(*69 145, 146, 149, 170*)
Length: 20 feet (6 meters)
Habitat: rivers and lakes
throughout Africa
Diet: fish, birds, turtles, and mammals –
almost any animal they can catch
Fact: A crocodile can stay submerged
for up to two hours.

crow (*107*)
Wingspan: 39 inches
(1 meter)
Habitat: temperate regions
worldwide, except for South America
Diet: insects, carrion, garbage, seeds,
and small animals
Fact: Crows sometimes use tools – a
twig or a piece of wire – to extract an
insect from a hole or crevice.

crucifix toad (*83*)
Length: 2½ inches
(6½ centimeters)
Habitat: dry regions of
Australia
Diet: ants, termites, and other insects
Fact: In dry weather this toad buries
itself in a cocoon that keeps it moist.
When it rains — sometimes weeks or
months later — the toad emerges and
searches for a mate.

Darwin's frog (*40*)
Length: 1 inch
(2½ centimeters)
Habitat: streams in South
America
Diet: insects and small animals
Fact: This frog was first described by
the naturalist Charles Darwin, who
encountered it on his voyage around
the world.

deathwatch beetle (*26*)
Length: ¼ inch
(6 millimeters)
Habitat: southern England
Diet: tree bark
Fact: These beetles damage wooden
furniture and buildings and are
considered a serious pest.

decorator crab (*91*)
Size (including legs):
5 inches (12½ centimeters)
across
Habitat: the Pacific coastal waters of
North America
Diet: algae, sponges, and small
crustaceans
Fact: When a decorator crab sheds its
old shell and grows a new one it moves
its decorations to its new shell.

deep-sea gulper eel (*79*)
Length: 31 inches
(79 centimeters)
Habitat: oceans worldwide
Diet: fish, shrimp, and plankton.
Fact: A light-producing organ at the end
of this fish's long tail acts as a lure to
attract prey.

deep-sea shrimp (*99*)
Length: 1 inch
(2½ centimeters)
Habitat: temperate oceans
worldwide
Diet: animal plankton
Fact: The glowing goo this shrimp
ejects is illuminated by light-producing
bacteria.

diamondback rattlesnake
(*50*)
Length: 5½ feet (1½ meters)
Habitat: southern and
western United States and South
America
Diet: mice, rabbits, and other small
mammals
Fact: Rattlesnakes shed their skin
three or four times a year. With each
shedding, a new rattle is added to the
snake's tail.

domestic dog
(*48, 61, 145, 148*)
Weight: 2–200 pounds
(1–91 kilograms)
Habitat: worldwide, wherever
humans live
Diet: dog food (meat, vegetables, and
grains); some dogs also hunt and eat
frogs, birds, and small mammals
Fact: All dog breeds are descended
from wolves that lived in East Asia.

dolphin (bottlenose dolphin)
(*83*)
Length: 12 feet (3½ meters)
Habitat: warm oceans
worldwide
Diet: fish and squid
Fact: A dolphin sleeps with one-half of
its brain at a time. The other half stays
awake and reminds the dolphin to
breathe.

dragonfly (blue-eyed darner)
(*71, 148, 171*)
Length: 2½ inches
(6½ centimeters)
Habitat: western North America
Diet: butterflies, moths, mosquitoes, and
other dragonflies
Fact: A dragonfly can swallow its body
weight in mosquitoes every day.

Dsungaripterus (*151*)
Wingspan: 10 feet (3 meters)
Habitat: China
(140 million years ago)
Diet: fish, clams, and other shellfish
Fact: This extinct flying reptile had teeth
and jaws strong enough to crush a
clamshell.

earwig (*33*)
Length: ½ inch
(13 millimeters)
Habitat: damp, dark
places worldwide
Diet: insects, plants, and garbage
Fact: There is a myth that earwigs
burrow into a person's ear and lay eggs
in their brain. Fortunately, this is untrue.

echidna (*32*)
Length: 16 inches
(41 centimeters)
Habitat: New Guinea
and Australia
Diet: ants and termites
Fact: The echidna's snout is sensitive to
the faint electrical fields created by the
bodies of the insects it feeds on.

Elasmotherium (*117*)
Length: 15 feet (4½ meters)
Habitat: plains of Eurasia
(until 50,000 years ago)
Diet: grass
Fact: This extinct prehistoric rhinoceros
had a horn as tall as a full-grown man.

electric eel (*64*)
Length: 8 feet (2½ meters)
Habitat: tropical rivers of
South America
Diet: fish and small mammals
Fact: This eel can produce an electrical
discharge of 600 volts, strong enough
to stun or kill a human.

elephant bird (*117*)
Height: 10 feet (3 meters)
Weight: 880 pounds
(400 kilograms)
Habitat: Madagascar (until the 1700s)
Diet: fruit
Fact: This bird was probably hunted to
extinction by humans.

MORE ANIMAL FACTS

elephant seal (*28*)
Length: 16 feet (5 meters)
Weight: 6,600 pounds
(3,000 kilograms)
Habitat: the Pacific coast of North America; the coasts of New Zealand, South America, and Africa
Diet: rays, squid, octopuses, and fish
Fact: Elephant seals spend 80 percent of their time in the water.

emperor penguin
(*41, 48, 142, 146*)
Height: 4 feet (1¼ meters)
Habitat: coastal Antarctica
Diet: fish, squid, and krill
Fact: An emperor penguin colony may contain ten of thousands of birds.

Etruscan shrew (*132*)
Length: 2 inches
(5 centimeters)
Habitat: Lands around the Mediterranean Sea; parts of India and Southeast Asia
Diet: earthworms, insects, spiders, and small reptiles and amphibians
Fact: This tiny shrew may eat 25 times a day, consuming twice its body weight every 24 hours.

European roller (*98*)
Length: 12 inches
(30 centimeters)
Habitat: Europe, the Middle East, and North Africa
Diet: insects, centipedes, spiders, worms, frogs, lizards, snakes, and birds
Fact: These birds migrate more than 12,000 miles (19,000 kilometers) every year.

European water vole (*141*)
Length (body): 6½ inches
(16½ centimeters)
Habitat: throughout Europe and northern Asia
Diet: grass, water plants, fruit, and roots
Fact: Water voles dig elaborate tunnel systems. There are multiple levels to prevent flooding and emergency exits both above and below the water.

eyelash viper (*91*)
Length: up to 30 inches
(76 centimeters)
Habitat: forests of Central and South America
Diet: mammals, lizards, frogs, and birds
Fact: This snake is not aggressive, but its bite can be deadly to humans.

fat-tailed scorpion (*145*)
Length: 4 inches
(10 centimeters)
Habitat: desert regions of the Middle East and Africa

Diet: crickets and other insects
Fact: Newly hatched baby scorpions — as many as 40 of them — cling to their mother's back for several days.

feather-horned beetle (*60*)
Length: ¾ inch
(2 centimeters)
Habitat: Australia
Diet: insect larvae
Fact: This beetle's elaborate antennae allow it to detect scents produced by other beetles from a great distance.

flame scallop (*89*)
Size: 3 inches
(7½ centimeters) across
Habitat: coral reefs in western Atlantic Ocean and Caribbean Sea
Diet: algae and small animals
Fact: This scallop gets its bright red color from pigments in the algae and plankton it feeds on.

flat-faced longhorn beetle (*17*)
Length: ¾ inch
(2 centimeters)
Habitat: Tanzania
Diet: flowers, pollen, and nectar
Fact: This beetle's antennae are more than twice the length of its body.

flying frog (*88*)
Length: 4 inches
(10 centimeters)
Habitat: forests and jungles of Southeast Asia
Diet: insects and other invertebrates
Fact: The flying frog can glide as far as 50 feet (15 meters).

four-eyed fish (*52*)
Length: 10 inches
(25 centimeters)
Habitat: rivers and streams in South America
Diet: insects, other invertebrates, and small fishes
Fact: The top half of this fish's eye is sensitive to green light, while the bottom half is sensitive to yellow light. This probably helps it both watch the sky (for predators) and see prey in the muddy, murky water in which it lives.

frilled lizard (*102*)
Length: 3 feet
(91 centimeters)
Habitat: forests and woodlands of Australia
Diet: ants, other lizards, spiders, and small mammals
Fact: This reptile's frill also helps regulate its body temperature.

fulmar gull (*99*)
Length (adult): 20 inches
(51 centimeters)
Habitat: rocky coasts of the northern and southern Atlantic and Pacific Oceans
Diet: krill, fish, and squid
Fact: Occasionally a human rock climber disturbs a fulmar gull chick. In return they get a face full of orange vomit that has a strong odor of rotten fish.

Galápagos tortoise
(*35, 140, 146, 148*)
Length: 5 feet (1½ meters)
Habitat: Galápagos Islands
Diet: leaves, seeds, and fruit
Fact: In the past, sailors took thousands of these tortoises on board their ships to serve as a source of food.

garden snail (*12*)
Length: 1½ inches
(4 centimeters)
Habitat: temperate and subtropical regions worldwide
Diet: fruits, leaves, and flowers
Fact: Snails are considered a delicacy in France, where they are cooked in their shells and eaten as an appetizer.

garter snake (*78*)
Length: 22 inches
(56 centimeters)
Habitat: North America
Diet: earthworms, lizards, ants, toads, and rodents
Fact: This snake is often seen in yards and gardens. It is harmless to humans.

geographic cone snail (*80*)
Length: 6 inches
(15 centimeters)
Habitat: coral reefs in the southwestern Pacific and Indian Oceans
Diet: worms, small fish, and mollusks
Fact: This shellfish is nicknamed the "cigarette snail" based on the belief that a person stung by one of these animals will only live long enough to smoke a cigarette — about 15 minutes.

giant anteater (*44, 126, 147*)
Length: 6½ feet
(2 meters)
Habitat: grasslands and forests of Central and South America
Diet: ants and termites
Fact: As it feeds, the giant anteater flicks its tongue in and out at a rate of three times a second.

giant barrel sponge (*141, 149*)
Size: up to 6 feet
(1¾ meters) across
Habitat: coral reefs and sandy sea floors in the Caribbean

Diet: bacteria, algae, and tiny animals
Fact: By filtering large quantities of water, sponges help keep their coral reef environment clean.

giant green anemone (*107*)
Size: up to 9 inches (23 centimeters) across
Habitat: coastal waters of the northeastern Pacific Ocean
Diet: crabs, fish, and other small marine creatures
Fact: This anemone has a symbiotic relationship with algae that live in its tissues. The algae provide some of the anemone's food through photosynthesis.

giant ground sloth (*163*)
Height: 20 feet (6 meters)
Weight: 8,500 pounds (3,855 kilograms)
Habitat: forests and grasslands of South America
Diet: grass and leaves
Fact: This elephant-size sloth became extinct about 10,000 years ago.

giant water bug (*41*)
Length: up to 4½ inches (11½ centimeters)
Habitat: freshwater streams and ponds worldwide
Diet: crustaceans, fish, and amphibians
Fact: This insect can give a person an extremely painful bite.

giraffe (*38, 49, 137, 147*)
Height: up to 18 feet (5½ meters)
Habitat: savannah and woodlands in central and southern Africa
Diet: leaves, shrubs, and grass
Fact: The giraffe's 20-inch (50-centimeter)-long tongue is dark purple to protect it against sunburn.

giraffe weevil (*28*)
Length: 1½ inch (4 centimeters)
Habitat: Madagascar
Diet: leaves of a tree known as the giraffe beetle tree
Fact: Using its long neck, the giraffe weevil can roll a leaf into a tube to make a nest for a single egg.

glass frog (*90*)
Length: 1 inch (2½ centimeters)
Habitat: trees near streams in the tropical forests of the Americas
Diet: spiders and insects
Fact: Glass frogs lay their eggs on leaves overhanging a stream. When the eggs hatch, the tadpoles drop into the water.

glowworm (*79*)
Length: 1½ inches (4 centimeters)
Habitat: caves in New Zealand and Australia
Diet: insects and small invertebrates
Fact: There is a famous glowworm cave in New Zealand that attracts thousand of visitors a year.

goby (*106*)
Length: up to 3 inches (7½ centimeters)
Habitat: warm Pacific Ocean waters and the Red Sea
Diet: plankton
Fact: Fins on the goby's belly act as suction cups, allowing the fish to hold on tightly to rocks or coral.

Goliath birdeater tarantula (*124*)
Size (including legs): 12 inches (30 centimeters) across
Habitat: swamps and marshes of northern South America
Diet: frogs, insects, lizards, rodents, and small birds
Fact: These spiders stalk their prey, pounce, and deliver a deadly bite with their venomous fangs.

gorilla (*43, 49, 147*)
Weight: as much as 600 pounds (272 kilograms)
Habitat: forests of central Africa
Diet: leaves, fruit, nuts, and roots
Fact: Gorillas live in a family group known as a troop.

grasshopper mouse (*72*)
Length (body): 5 inches (12½ centimeters)
Habitat: dry regions of western North America
Diet: insects, lizards, and other mice
Fact: When it makes a kill, this mouse stands on its hind legs, throws back its head, and howls.

great crested grebe (*31*)
Length: 20 inches (51 centimeters)
Habitat: rivers, lakes, and ponds throughout Europe and Asia
Diet: fish, frogs, crayfish, and insects
Fact: Young crested grebes can swim almost as soon as they hatch.

great white shark (*65, 67, 111, 144, 146, 148*)
Length: 20 feet (6 meters)
Weight: 5,000 pounds (2,268 kilograms)
Habitat: cool coastal waters worldwide

Diet: seals, sea lions, fish, squid, and — rarely — humans.
Fact: These sharks have as many as 3,000 teeth. They are continually falling out and being replaced by new teeth.

green basilisk lizard (*88*)
Length: 2 feet (61 centimeters)
Habitat: rainforests of Central America
Diet: insects, fruit, and small animals
Fact: This lizard gets the nickname "Jesus Christ lizard" from a story in the Bible in which Jesus walks on water.

green June beetle (*13*)
Length: 1 inch (2½ centimeters)
Habitat: North America
Diet: fruit
Fact: This beetle is a pest — it damages fruit grown for human consumption.

green vine snake (*74*)
Length: 6½ feet (2 meters)
Habitat: Central America and northern South America
Diet: rodents, lizards, frogs, and birds
Fact: Although this snake is mildly venomous, it is sometimes kept as a pet.

grizzly bear (*71*)
Weight: 600 pounds (272 kilograms)
Habitat: the northwestern United States and western Canada
Diet: berries, fruit, roots, rodents, deer, elk, and moose
Fact: Female grizzlies normally give birth to two cubs every three or four years.

hairy angler (*31*)
Length (female): 1 foot (30 centimeters)
Length (male): 1¼ inch (3 centimeters)
Habitat: deep ocean waters worldwide
Diet: fish and shrimp
Fact: The female hairy angler attracts its prey with a glowing lure on the end of a long stalk.

hairy frog (*105*)
Length: 4½ inches (11½ centimeters)
Habitat: central Africa
Diet: slugs, spiders, and insects
Fact: The hairy projections on the body of this frog act as gills, absorbing oxygen when it is in the water.

hatchet fish (*90*)
Length: 4 inches (10 centimeters)
Habitat: deep tropical waters

of the Atlantic, Pacific, and Indian Oceans
Diet: shrimp and small fish
Fact: This fish has a body shaped like a hatchet blade. It is so thin that it almost disappears when viewed head-on.

hermit crab (*106*)
Length: 4 inches
(10 centimeters)
Habitat: shallow ocean waters worldwide
Diet: plants, worms, and small animals
Fact: There are more than 1,000 species of hermit crab, including some that live on land. The hermit crab in this book is a common ocean-dwelling variety.

herring gull (*82*)
Length: 24 inches
(61 centimeters)
Habitat: coastal North America and northern Europe
Diet: fish, crabs, worms, shellfish, insects, and small birds
Fact: Some herring gulls, also known as seagulls, live in coastal cities where they nest on the roofs of buildings.

hippopotamus (*144*)
Weight: 6,000 pounds
(2,720 kilograms)
Habitat: rivers and lakes in central and southern Africa
Diet: grass and water plants
Fact: Hippos are easily sunburned, so they spend much of the daylight hours partly submerged.

hog-nosed snake (*103*)
Length: 4 feet (1¼ meters)
Habitat: the United States and northern Mexico
Diet: rodents and lizards
Fact: Before the hog-nosed snake resorts to playing dead, it tries to frighten a predator away by puffing itself up and hissing loudly.

honeybee (*52*)
Length: ½ inch
(13 millimeters)
Habitat: temperate regions worldwide
Diet: flower pollen and nectar
Fact: Hundreds of years ago, settlers brought honeybees to North America from Europe.

hooded pitohui (*95*)
Length: 8 inches
(20 centimeters)
Habitat: New Guinea
Diet: beetles and other insects
Fact: Touching this bird's feathers can cause numbness and tingling.

hooded seal (*27*)
Length: 8 feet (2½ meters)
Weight: up to 900 pounds
(408 kilograms)
Habitat: ice and open water in the northern Atlantic Ocean
Diet: fish and squid
Fact: These seals can hold their breath for as long as fifty minutes.

horned lizard (*99*)
Length: 4 inches
(10 centimeters)
Habitat: the southwestern United States and Mexico
Diet: ants and other insects
Fact: The "horns" around this lizard's head are positioned in such a way that rainwater falling on the lizard's body is directed into its mouth.

housecat (*58, 119, 148*)
Weight: 10 pounds
(4½ kilograms)
Habitat: almost everywhere that humans live
Diet: canned or dry cat food, rodents, birds, amphibians, reptiles, fish, and invertebrates
Fact: Cats are the most popular pet in the world. They were probably domesticated at least 10,000 years ago.

housefly
(*13, 16, 48, 60, 67, 141, 148*)
Length: ¼ inch (6 millimeters)
Habitat: everywhere that humans live
Diet: garbage, human food, animal waste, and carrion
Fact: Houseflies carry many diseases that can be transmitted to humans.

howler monkey (*138*)
Length: 30 inches
(76 centimeters)
Habitat: rainforests of Central and South America
Diet: leaves, fruit, and flowers
Fact: The howler monkey has a prehensile tail — a tail that can be used like an extra hand.

humpback whale (*56*)
Length: 50 feet (15 meters)
Habitat: oceans worldwide
Diet: plankton
Fact: Humpbacks migrate about 16,000 miles (29,600 kilometers) every year.

ichneumon wasp (*33*)
Size: 2 inches
(5 centimeters)
Habitat: forests in North America
Diet: Adults do not eat. The larvae are parasites — they feed on the larvae of other insects.
Fact: The female wasp has a 4-inch (10-centimeter)-long egg-laying organ called an ovipositor. It can drill a hole in solid wood.

Indian rhinoceros (*97*)
Length: 12 feet (3½ meters)
Weight: 4,500 pounds
(2,040 kilograms)
Habitat: northern India and Nepal
Diet: grass, leaves, and shrubs
Fact: There are only about 2,500 of these animals left in the wild.

Indricotherium (*116*)
Weight: 18 tons
(16,330 kilograms)
Habitat: eastern Europe and Asia (30 million years ago)
Diet: leaves of trees and shrubs
Fact: This huge herbivore was the largest land mammal that has ever lived.

ironclad beetle (*93*)
Length: 1 inch
(2½ centimeters)
Habitat: the southwestern United States and Mexico
Diet: fungi growing on dead wood
Fact: As their name suggests, these beetles have extremely hard exoskeletons. Insect collectors must drill a hole before they can push a pin through this beetle's body.

Jackson's chameleon (*52*)
Length: 9 inches
(23 centimeters)
Habitat: forests of eastern Africa
Diet: insects and worms
Fact: Chameleons change color not to camouflage themselves, but to reflect or absorb sunlight, respond to changes in temperature, or communicate with other chameleons.

jaguar (*75*)
Weight: 300 pounds
(136 kilograms)
Habitat: southern Mexico and northern South America
Diet: deer, wild pigs, lizards, fish, and other small animals
Fact: The jaguar is the world's third largest cat — the lion and tiger are larger.

Japanese flying squid (*89*)
Length: 18 inches
(46 centimeters)
Habitat: the northern Pacific Ocean
Diet: fish, shrimp, plankton, and squid
Fact: The flying squid propels itself by forcing a jet of water through a tube on the underside of its head.

Japanese honeybee (*106*)
See *honeybee*

jewel beetle (*64*)
Length: 2 inches
(5 centimeters)
Habitat: New Guinea
Diet: plant material
Fact: This is one of 15,000 species of jewel beetles. The hard, colorful wing coverings of these insects are sometimes used to make jewelry.

jumping spider (*52*)
Size (including legs): ¼ inch (six millimeters) across
Habitat: temperate and tropical regions worldwide
Diet: insects and spiders
Fact: There are more than 5,000 species of jumping spider. All have keen eyesight, and they chase or stalk their prey rather than building webs.

kakapo (*138*)
Length: 24 inches
(61 centimeters)
Habitat: New Zealand
Diet: leaves, seeds, and fruits
Fact: The kakapo is critically endangered — there are only about 100 of these flightless birds living in the wild.

kangaroo rat (*142*)
Length (body): 3 inches
(7½ centimeters)
Habitat: dry regions of the western United States
Diet: seeds and grasses
Fact: The kangaroo rat spends its days sleeping in an underground burrow.

kestrel (*53*)
Length: 15 inches
(38 centimeters)
Habitat: Africa, Asia, and Europe
Diet: voles, shrews, and mice
Fact: Kestrels catch and eat as many as eight rodents a day.

king cobra (*29*)
Length: 18 feet (5½ meters)
Habitat: India, southern China, and Southeast Asia
Diet: other snakes, lizards, birds, eggs, and small mammals
Fact: This is the world's longest venomous snake. Its hiss is so low that it sounds like a growl.

kiwi (*60*)
Weight: 6 pounds
(2¾ kilograms)
Habitat: forests of New Zealand
Diet: worms, insects, leaves, and fruit

Fact: A female kiwi lays a single large egg each year.

koi (*141*)
Length: 3 feet
(91 centimeters)
Habitat: every continent except Antarctica
Diet: fish food, insects, and water plants
Fact: Koi have been bred from carp. If released into the wild, they lose their decorative coloration and become ordinary carp within a few generations.

krait (*145*)
Length: 5 feet (1½ meters)
Habitat: India and Sri Lanka
Diet: other snakes, lizards, frogs, rats, and mice
Fact: The krait is active at night. It sometimes bites humans who are sleeping, and its venom is so deadly that people bitten in this way often never wake up.

leaf beetle (*17*)
Length: ¼ inch (6 millimeters)
Habitat: Brazil
Diet: leaves
Fact: This tiny leaf beetle lives in South America, but there are 35,000 other species of leaf beetle, found almost everywhere on earth.

leafy seadragon (*93*)
Length: 10 inches
(25 centimeters)
Habitat: ocean kelp beds off the south and west coasts of Australia
Diet: shrimp, plankton, and small fish
Fact: A male seadragon carries the eggs laid by his mate until they hatch.

leatherback sea turtle
(*120, 146*)
Length: 7 feet (2 meters)
Weight: up to 2,000 pounds (907 kilograms)
Habitat: oceans worldwide
Diet: jellyfish
Fact: Leatherback turtles have a soft rubbery shell rather than a hard bony one.

lightning bug (*79*)
Length: 1 inch
(2½ centimeters)
Habitat: temperate and tropical regions worldwide
Diet: other lightning bugs, nectar, pollen, or nothing at all — some lightning bugs do not feed as adults
Fact: Thousands of these insects, which are also known as fireflies, will sometimes alight in the same tree and flash in unison.

lion's mane jellyfish (*136*)
Length (tentacles): 120 feet
(36½ meters)
Habitat: the Arctic, northern Atlantic, and Pacific Oceans
Diet: zooplankton, small fish, shrimp, and other jellyfish
Fact: Despite their size, these jellyfish live for only about one year.

little brown bat (*57, 67*)
Wingspan: 11 inches
(28 centimeters)
Habitat: throughout North America
Diet: moths, mosquitoes, and other flying insects
Fact: These bats can eat half their body weight in insects every night.

long-tailed weasel (*74*)
Length (including tail):
13 inches (33 centimeters)
Habitat: southern Canada, the United States, Central America, and northern South America
Diet: birds, mice, rabbits, and other small mammals
Fact: This weasel can kill and eat animals much larger than itself.

long-wattled umbrella bird
(*27*)
Length: 18 inches
(46 centimeters)
Habitat: rainforests of South America
Diet: fruit, insects, frogs, and lizards
Fact: In addition to displaying its plumage, the male makes a low rumbling sound when it's courting a female.

Malaysian ant (*100*)
Size: ¼ inch (6 millimeters)
Habitat: Malaysia
Diet: insects and plant nectar
Fact: By rupturing its toxin sacs and exploding itself, this ant sacrifices itself to preserve its colony.

Malaysian cherry-red centipede (*94*)
Length: 8 inches
(20 centimeters)
Habitat: forests of Southeast Asia
Diet: insects, spiders, frogs, mice, and other small animals
Fact: The bite of this large centipede is very painful to humans, and can cause serious swelling and fever.

manatee (*39, 58*)
Length: 12 feet (3½ meters)
Habitat: coastal waters and rivers of the southeastern United States, the Caribbean, the Amazon River basin, and West Africa

Diet: leaves and water plants
Fact: Manatees, also called sea cows, have no natural enemies. Unfortunately, many are killed in collisions with boats.

mantis shrimp (*82*)
Length: 12 inches (30 centimeters)
Habitat: warm ocean waters worldwide
Diet: crabs, snails, fish, and clams
Fact: The strike of a mantis shrimp is one of the fastest movements in the animal world. These shrimp are called "thumb splitters" for the damage they can do to an unwary diver's hand.

margay (*78*)
Weight: 7 pounds (3 kilograms)
Habitat: forests of Central and South America
Diet: monkeys, small mammals, birds, eggs, lizards, and frogs
Fact: The margay is an excellent climber. It can hang from a branch using one foot.

marine iguana (*3*)
Length: 5 feet (1½ meters)
Habitat: Galápagos Islands
Diet: algae and seaweed
Fact: Marine iguanas can stay underwater for as long as one hour.

mayfly (*141, 148*)
Size: ½ inch (13 millimeters)
Habitat: near lakes and streams in temperate and tropical parts of the world
Diet: Adult mayflies do not eat.
Fact: A mayfly larva may live for a year, but as an adult, it has a very short life — 30 minutes to a few days.

megalodon (*110*)
Length: 52 feet (16 meters)
Habitat: oceans worldwide
Diet: whales, dolphins, squid, fish, and marine reptiles
Fact: Megalodon lived from 28 million to about 1½ million years ago. It was one of the largest predators of all time.

metallic green weevil (*17*)
Length: ¼ inch (6 millimeters)
Habitat: Polynesia
Diet: yam leaves
Fact: This toxic beetle acquires its poisons from the yam plants it eats.

Mexican beaded lizard (*81*)
Length: 30 inches (76 centimeters)
Habitat: forests and scrublands of Central America
Diet: bird and reptile eggs, birds, mammals, frogs, and insects

Fact: This large venomous lizard climbs trees to raid birds' nests.

mole cricket (*138*)
Length: 1½ inches (4 centimeters)
Habitat: grasslands on every continent except Antarctica
Diet: plant roots and stems, worms, and insect larvae
Fact: In some parts of Asia, people use these crickets as food.

monarch butterfly (*92*)
Wingspan: 4 inches (10 centimeters)
Habitat: North America, South America, and New Zealand
Diet: flower nectar
Fact: Monarch larvae eat only milkweed plants. It is this diet that makes both the larva and the adult butterfly toxic and foul tasting to birds and other predators.

Morgan's sphinx moth (*137*)
Wingspan: 5 inches (12½ centimeters)
Habitat: East Africa and Madagascar
Diet: orchid nectar
Fact: Based on the discovery of an orchid that could be pollinated only by an insect with a very long tongue, the existence of this moth was predicted years before it was found.

mosquito (*17, 145*)
Length: ½ inch (13 millimeters)
Habitat: every continent except Antarctica
Diet: nectar and blood
Fact: Only female mosquitoes feed on blood.

mother-of-pearl moth caterpillar (*89*)
Length: ¾ inch (2 centimeters)
Habitat: Europe
Diet: stinging nettle
Fact: As it rolls away to escape danger, this caterpillar moves 40 times faster than it can crawl.

myna bird (*47*)
Length: 9 inches (23 centimeters)
Habitat: Native to India and Southeast Asia, it has been introduced to North America and Australia
Diet: insects and fruit
Fact: Mynas can mimic human speech.

naked mole rat (*65*)
Length: 3½ inches (9 centimeters)
Habitat: the grasslands of

eastern Africa
Diet: tubers and roots
Fact: Naked mole rats are also called sand puppies. They are the only cold-blooded mammals.

narwhal (*136*)
Length (body): 13 feet (4 meters)
Length (tusk): up to 18 feet (5½ meters)
Habitat: the Arctic Ocean
Diet: fish and squid
Fact: Hundreds of years ago, narwhal tusks brought to Europe by the Vikings were thought to prove the existence of the unicorn, a mythical creature.

nautilus (*96*)
Size: 8 inches across (20 centimeters)
Habitat: the Indo-Pacific Ocean
Diet: crabs, shrimp, and fish
Fact: The nautilus comes from an ancient line of animals that has changed little in 500 million years.

New Mexico whiptail lizard (*25*)
Length: 9 inches (23 centimeters)
Habitat: the southwestern United States and northern Mexico
Diet: insects
Fact: These lizards can run at speeds of 15 miles (24 kilometers) per hour.

nine-banded armadillo (*39, 102*)
Length: 30 inches (76 centimeters)
Habitat: South America and the southern United States
Diet: worms, grubs, and insects
Fact: An armadillo can cross a stream by emptying its lungs and walking across on the bottom.

oarfish (*137, 146*)
Size: 50 feet (15 meters)
Habitat: deep ocean waters worldwide
Diet: plankton, small fish, and jellyfish
Fact: These deep-water fish are seldom seen alive. Most of what we know about them comes from dead oarfish that have washed up on the shore.

ocean sunfish (*32*)
Length: 10 feet (3 meters)
Weight: up to 5,000 pounds (2,268 kilograms)
Habitat: warm ocean waters worldwide
Diet: jellyfish and plankton
Fact: This huge fish is also known as a mola mola.

octopus (giant Pacific octopus) (*60*)
Length: 20 feet (6 meters)
Habitat: coastal waters of the northern Pacific Ocean
Diet: shrimp, crabs, clams, and fish
Fact: The octopus is an intelligent animal. In captivity it can solve puzzles and mazes. It is also good at escaping from its tank.

orchid mantis (*75*)
Length (female): 2½ inches (6½ centimeters)
Habitat: rainforests of Southeast Asia
Diet: insects, small lizards
Fact: Over a period of days, an orchid mantis will change color to match its surroundings.

ostrich (*22*)
Height: 9 feet (2¾ meters)
Habitat: grasslands and savannahs of Africa
Diet: grasses, shrubs, seeds, and insects
Fact: The flightless ostrich can run almost as fast as a racehorse.

Paedocypris (*133*)
Length: 5/16 inch (8 millimeters)
Habitat: swamps in Southeast Asia
Diet: rotifers and other microscopic animals
Fact: Decomposing plant material makes the water in which these fish live as acidic as vinegar.

pangolin (*97*)
Length: 36 inches (91 centimeters)
Habitat: tropical regions of Africa and Asia
Diet: ants and termites
Fact: The pangolin's scales are made of keratin — the same material as our fingernails.

parent bug (*42*)
Length: 3/8 inch (9 millimeters)
Habitat: northern Europe and the British Isles
Diet: tree sap
Fact: The male parent bug dies soon after mating, but the mother usually survives and takes care of her babies.

Patu digua (*133*)
Length (males): 1/80 inch (1/3 millimeter)
Habitat: northern South America
Diet: small insects

Fact: Male spiders are typically much smaller than females. Since female spiders of some other species are only slightly larger than the male patu digua, it's likely that there are even smaller male spiders yet to be discovered.

pebble toad (*89*)
Length: 1 inch (2½ centimeters)
Habitat: mountains of the Amazonian rainforest
Diet: insects
Fact: These toads nest in groups. There may be more than 100 baby toads in a single nest.

pelican (*42*)
Wingspan: up to 8 feet (2½ meters)
Habitat: Atlantic, Pacific, and Gulf Coasts
Diet: fish and crustaceans
Fact: Pelicans have the largest bills of any bird.

peregrine falcon (*46*)
Length: 18 inches (46 centimeters)
Habitat: every continent except Antarctica
Diet: birds, small mammals, and reptiles
Fact: Peregrine falcons can live in cities. They nest on tall buildings and hunt city birds such as pigeons and sparrows.

pike (northern) (*72*)
Length: up to 5 feet (1½ meters)
Habitat: freshwater lakes, ponds, and marshes throughout the northern hemisphere
Diet: fish, frogs, ducklings, and small mammals
Fact: The pike has motion sensors on its skin that help it find prey in dark or murky water.

pistol shrimp (*139*)
Length: 1½ inches (4 centimeters)
Habitat: warm, shallow seas worldwide
Diet: shrimp, crabs, and fish
Fact: This shrimp can produce a sound that is louder than a gunshot.

platypus (*94*)
Length: 20 inches (50 centimeters)
Habitat: eastern Australia
Diet: insects and small animals
Fact: The platypus has receptors on its bill that can detect the faint electrical fields created by its prey.

poison dart frog (*95*)
Length: 2 inches (5 centimeters)
Habitat: rainforests of Central and South America
Diet: ants, termites, and beetles
Fact: Native people in the rainforest roast this frog over a fire, then dip the tips of their blowgun darts in the poison that oozes from its skin.

Polynesian megapode (*33*)
Length: 15 inches (38 centimeters)
Habitat: two small volcanic islands in the South Pacific Ocean
Diet: insects, lizards, seeds, and fruit
Fact: Human hunting and egg collecting threaten these birds — there are only about 1,000 left.

Pompeii worm (*142*)
Length: 5 inches (12½ centimeters)
Habitat: deep sea hydrothermal vents in the Pacific Ocean
Diet: microorganisms
Fact: This worm holds its tail in the plume of scalding hot water coming from a volcanic vent. At the same time, it keeps its head in much cooler water.

porcupine (*96*)
Length: 30 inches (76 centimeters)
Habitat: North and South America, southern Asia, and Africa
Diet: leaves, twigs, and bark
Fact: A porcupine may have more than 30,000 quills.

praying mantis (*76*)
Length: up to 6 inches (15 centimeters)
Habitat: warm and tropical regions worldwide
Diet: insects, lizards, mice, and small birds
Fact: The praying mantis gets its name from its habit of holding its arms folded in front of its body, as if in prayer.

Prionosuchus (*114*)
Length: 30 feet (9 meters)
Habitat: South America (270 million years ago)
Diet: fish and other aquatic animals
Fact: This giant amphibian was probably an ambush hunter, lunging and grabbing when its prey got close enough.

pronghorn antelope (*88*)
Height (at the shoulder): 36 inches (91 centimeters)
Habitat: central and western North America

Diet: grass, leaves, and cacti
Fact: This antelope is the second fastest land animal. The cheetah is faster, but the pronghorn can maintain its speed for a much greater distance.

 pufferfish (*97*)
Length: 12 inches (30 centimeters)
Habitat: warm ocean waters worldwide
Diet: algae and shellfish
Fact: A single pufferfish contains enough toxin to kill 30 adult humans.

 pygmy mouse lemur (*131*)
Length (body): 2½ inches (6 centimeters)
Habitat: forests of Madagascar
Diet: fruit, flowers, and nectar
Fact: The pygmy mouse lemur's large eyes help it see at night, when it is active. It sleeps during the day.

 quahog clam (*141, 149*)
Length: 4 inches (10 centimeters)
Habitat: eastern shores of North America
Diet: algae and small organic particles
Fact: A quahog's age can be determined by counting the rings on its shell — one ring is added each year.

 Quetzalcoatlus (*115*)
Wingspan: 36 feet (11 meters)
Habitat: North America (67 million years ago)
Diet: small animals
Fact: Soaring on thermal updrafts, this flying reptile could probably stay aloft for days.

 red-eyed tree frog (*103*)
Length: 2 inches (5 centimeters)
Habitat: Mexico, Central America, and northern South America
Diet: crickets, flies, and other insects
Fact: These frogs sleep while attached to the bottom of a leaf.

 red spitting cobra (*98*)
Length: 3½ feet (1 meter)
Habitat: East Africa
Diet: frogs, birds, small mammals, and other snakes
Fact: The bite of this cobra can be fatal to humans.

 reticulated python (*122, 147*)
Length: up to 25 feet (7½ meters)
Habitat: Southeast Asia
Diet: monkeys, pigs, birds, and small mammals

Fact: These snakes are excellent swimmers and have been spotted in the ocean far from land.

 ring-necked snake (*122*)
Length: 1 foot (30 centimeters)
Habitat: the United States, Mexico, and southeastern Canada
Diet: worms, frogs, lizards, and other snakes
Fact: When threatened, this mildly venomous snake rolls over to reveal a bright red or yellow belly. Since many poisonous animals are brightly colored, this can discourage a predator.

 rotifer (*Euchlanis*) (*134*)
Length: ¹/₅₀₀ inch (¹/₂₀ millimeter)
Habitat: freshwater ponds and marshes
Diet: dead bacteria, algae, and protozoans
Fact: This tiny animal has a transparent, glasslike shell.

 rufous woodpecker (*107*)
Length: 9 inches (23 centimeters)
Habitat: India and Southeast Asia
Diet: ants, other insects, fruit, and sap
Fact: Black ants normally eat birds' eggs, and ants are a normal part of this bird's diet. When the woodpecker lays her eggs in the ants' nest, however, they do not attack each other.

 Rüppell's vulture (*143*)
Wingspan: 8 feet (2½ meters)
Habitat: desert regions of central Africa
Diet: dead animals
Fact: These vultures will devour the skin — even the bones — of a carcass once all the flesh has been consumed.

 sailfish (*70*)
Length: 10 feet (3 meters)
Habitat: warm and temperate oceans worldwide
Diet: fish and squid
Fact: Sailfish can rapidly change color, turning purple, gray, or silver — even light blue with yellow stripes. They do this to confuse prey and to communicate with other sailfish.

 Sally Lightfoot crab (*3*)
Size: 3 inches (7½ centimeters) across
Habitat: rocky shores of the Atlantic and Pacific coasts of South America, the Pacific coast of North America, and the Galápagos Islands

Diet: algae, dead fish and birds, ticks and dead skin of the marine iguana
Fact: This crab is alert, agile, and difficult for a predator to catch.

 saluki (*70*)
Weight: 50 pounds (23 kilograms)
Habitat: originally bred in Egypt, now domesticated worldwide
Diet: dog food, meat, and small animals (if the saluki is allowed to hunt)
Fact: The saluki was the royal dog of ancient Egypt. Mummified salukis have been found buried alongside Egyptian pharaohs.

 satanic leaf-tailed gecko (*86*)
Length: 4 inches (10 centimeters)
Habitat: Madagascar
Diet: insects
Fact: If its camouflage fails, this lizard will try to frighten off a predator by hissing and displaying the inside of its bright red mouth.

 scorpion fly (*30*)
Length: 1 inch (2½ centimeters)
Habitat: temperate and subtropical climates worldwide
Diet: dead insects, nectar, and pollen
Fact: The scorpion fly gets its name from the male's abdomen, which curls over its back and resembles the stinger of a scorpion. The scorpion fly, however, does not sting.

 seahorse (*40*)
Length: ½ inch to 14 inches (1¼ to 36 centimeters)
Habitat: shallow tropical and temperate waters worldwide
Diet: plankton and small animals
Fact: Seahorses have no stomach. Food passes through their system quickly, and they have to eat almost constantly.

 sea krait (*80*)
Length: 30 inches (76 centimeters)
Habitat: the western Pacific Ocean and the eastern Indian Ocean
Diet: fish
Fact: The human victims of this ocean-dwelling snake are often fishermen who entangle the snake in their nets.

 sea urchin (purple sea urchin) (*141, 148*)
Size: up to 3 inches (7½ centimeters) across
Habitat: the Pacific coastal waters of North America
Diet: algae, decayed plants and animals

Fact: If a predator approaches, sea urchins point their spines in the direction of the threat.

Shastasaurus (*115*)
Length: 69 feet (21 meters)
Habitat: Oceans in the present location of the United States, Canada, and China (210 million years ago)
Diet: probably fish, squid, and other soft-bodied animals
Fact: This marine reptile had no teeth. It fed by sucking in its prey and swallowing it whole.

shrew (northern short-tailed shrew) (*42*)
Length (body): 4 inches (10 centimeters)
Habitat: forests and meadows in central and eastern North America
Diet: insects, worms, lizards, frogs, mice, seeds, and fungi
Fact: This shrew's saliva is toxic, making it one of the few venomous mammals.

Siamese fighting fish (*29*)
Length: 3 inches (7½ centimeters)
Habitat: originally native to Southeast Asia
Diet (in the wild): insects, insect larvae, and plankton
Fact: The male fish builds a bubble nest with his saliva. When the female lays her eggs, the male takes them in his mouth and places them in the nest. He keeps the female away, or she will devour her own eggs.

Siberian tiger (*119, 128, 146*)
Length (including tail): up to 13½ feet (4 meters)
Habitat: forests of far-eastern Russia and northeastern China
Diet: wild pigs, deer, elk, and bear; also frogs, snakes, and small mammals if larger prey is unavailable
Fact: The Siberian tiger is protected, but it is hunted illegally, often for use in traditional Chinese medical treatments. There are only about 300 of these animals left in the wild.

sifaka (*43*)
Height: 18 inches (46 centimeters)
Habitat: Madagascar
Diet: fruit, leaves, and bark
Fact: Sifakas spend most of their lives in the trees, and their feet are adapted for climbing, not walking. When a sifaka comes down to the ground, it moves in a series of graceful sideways leaps.

slow loris (*95*)
Length: 8 inches (20 centimeters)
Habitat: tropical forests of southern India and Sri Lanka
Diet: insects and fruit
Fact: The slow loris sleeps in a tree during the day with its arms wrapped around its head.

smelt (*58*)
Length: 8 inches (20 centimeters)
Habitat: coastal waters of the Atlantic and Pacific Oceans
Diet: shrimp, worms, small fish
Fact: Smelt spend most of their lives in the ocean but swim up rivers and streams to lay their eggs in fresh water.

solenodon (*81*)
Length (nose to tail): 20 inches (51 centimeters)
Habitat: Cuba and the West Indies
Diet: insects, worms, carrion, and small animals
Fact: The solenodon has a joint at the base of its nose that allows it to swivel its snout as it sniffs about for food.

sperm whale (*143, 176*)
Length: 60 feet (18 meters)
Weight: 55 tons (50,000 kilograms)
Habitat: oceans worldwide
Diet: squid, fish, and rays
Fact: A sperm whale in a deep dive can stay underwater for 90 minutes.

spicebush swallowtail butterfly caterpillar (*92*)
Length (caterpillar): 1½ inches (4 centimeters)
Wingspan (adult): 4 inches (10 centimeters)
Habitat: central and eastern United States and southeastern Canada
Diet: nectar
Fact: To create a nest, this caterpillar snips a leaf, rolls it into a cylinder, and glues it together.

spine-tailed swift (*71*)
Length: 9 inches (23 centimeters)
Habitat: throughout most of the world
Diet: flying insects
Fact: The spine-tailed swift has been clocked at 106 miles (170 kilometers) per hour in level flight.

Spinosaurus (*112*)
Length: 50 feet (15 meters)
Habitat: what is now North Africa (110 million years ago)

Diet: fish, carrion, and other animals
Fact: The sail on this dinosaur's back was probably used to help regulate its temperature. Its display may also have helped attract a mate.

spiny orb web spider (*97*)
Size (female): ½ inch (13 millimeters) across
Habitat: the southern United States, Central America, and South America
Diet: small insects
Fact: When a male approaches the much larger female to mate, he uses a special signal: he taps on one of her web's silk threads four times.

spotted turtle (*121*)
Length: 4 inches (10 centimeters)
Habitat: swamps, marshes, and streams in southern Canada and the eastern United States
Diet: water plants, algae, insects and insect larva, frogs, and small fish
Fact: These turtles may live to be 50 years old.

stag beetle (*29, 205*)
Length: 3½ inches (9 centimeters)
Habitat: Southeast Asia
Diet: tree sap
Fact: The male beetle does not use its antlers to sting or bite. They are used only for fighting other males.

starfish (*24*)
Size: 4 to 20 inches (10 to 50 centimeters) across
Habitat: sea floors worldwide
Diet: clams and other shellfish, sea cucumbers, sea urchins, coral polyps
Fact: Starfish, or sea stars, may have as few as 5 or as many as 40 arms.

starnose mole (*59*)
Length: 7 inches (18 centimeters)
Habitat: eastern Canada and the northeastern United States
Diet: insects, worms, mollusks, frogs, and small fish
Fact: The starnose mole can smell underwater.

stingray (*104*)
Size: up to 6½ feet (2 meters) across
Habitat: warm, shallow ocean waters worldwide
Diet: crabs, clams, shrimp, and small fish
Fact: The stingray ambushes prey and hides from predators by burying itself in the sand with only its eyes sticking out.

stonefish (*74*)
Length: 14 inches (36 centimeters)
Habitat: shallow tropical seas in the Indo-Pacific Ocean
Diet: fish and shrimp
Fact: The row of spines on the stonefish's back contain a potent toxin, protecting this fish against predators.

stoplight loosejaw (*53*)
Length: 6 inches (15 centimeters)
Habitat: deep ocean waters worldwide
Diet: fish and zooplankton
Fact: This fish can swallow prey larger than its own body.

Surinam toad (*38*)
Length: 7 inches (18 centimeters)
Habitat: South America
Diet: fish
Fact: The Surinam toad locates its prey by touch — each of its toes ends in five sensitive appendages.

tailorbird (*32*)
Length: 5 inches (12½ centimeters)
Habitat: India and Southeast Asia
Diet: insects, fruit, and nuts
Fact: This bird often makes its nest in urban parks and gardens.

tapir (Malayan) (*91*)
Length (adult): 7 feet (2 meters)
Weight: 650 pounds (295 kilograms)
Habitat: tropical forests of Southeast Asia
Diet: plant roots, stems, and leaves
Fact: The tapir uses its long, flexible snout to root through litter on the forest floor and find food.

tarsier (*164*)
Length (head and body): 5 inches (12½ centimeters)
Habitat: Southeast Asia
Diet: insects, spiders, lizards, and birds
Fact: Each of the tarsier's eyes is as big as its entire brain.

tawny owl (*56*)
Length: 18 inches (46 centimeters)
Habitat: forests in Europe and Asia
Diet: rodents, rabbits, birds, worms, and insects
Fact: Tawny owl parents mate for life.

tenrec (*56*)
Length (body): 2 inches (5 centimeters)
Habitat: Madagascar and parts of Africa
Diet: earthworms and insects
Fact: The tenrec produces a high-pitched squeak by rubbing its spines together. This sound is used to communicate with other tenrecs.

termite (*36*)
Length (worker): ¼ inch (6 millimeters)
Length (queen): up to 5 inches (12½ centimeters)
Habitat: every continent except Antarctica
Diet: wood, plant material, and fungi
Fact: In some parts of the world, people eat termite queens.

terror bird (*163*)
Height: 10 feet (3 meters)
Weight: 500 pounds (230 kilograms)
Habitat: Argentina (15 million years ago)
Diet: mammals, reptiles, other birds, and perhaps carrion
Fact: This bird was the dominant South American land predator of its time.

three-toed sloth (*90*)
Length: 18 inches (46 centimeters)
Habitat: rainforests of Central and South America
Diet: leaves and buds
Fact: This sloth may be the slowest of all mammals. In a hurry, it moves at a speed of 13 feet (4 meters) per minute.

tiger beetle (six-spotted green tiger beetle) (*70*)
Length: ½ inch (13 millimeters)
Habitat: throughout much of North America
Diet: caterpillars, ants, spiders, and other insects
Fact: The tiger beetle releases a foul-smelling liquid as a defense against predators.

tiger moth (*103*)
Wingspan: 2 inches (5 centimeters)
Habitat: throughout much of North America, Europe, and Asia
Diet (caterpillar): leaves, including those of many toxic plants
Diet (adult): flower nectar
Fact: Plant toxins accumulate in the tissues of the caterpillar, making it — and the adult moth — poisonous to many predators.

titan beetle (*125*)
Length: 6½ inches (16½ centimeters)
Habitat: rainforests of South America
Diet (larva): wood and decomposing plant material
Diet (adult): Adult titan beetles do not feed.
Fact: This beetle makes a loud hissing noise if threatened.

tortoise beetle (mottled tortoise beetle) (*96*)
Length: ¼ inch (6 millimeters)
Habitat: temperate regions of the United States and Canada
Diet: leaves
Fact: To hide from birds and other predators, the tortoise beetle covers its body with its own droppings.

trapdoor spider (*72*)
Body length: 1 inch (2½ centimeters)
Habitat: southern and western United States
Diet: insects, other spiders, and lizards
Fact: The trapdoor spider protects itself by bracing its legs against the sides of its burrow and grasping a special "handle" on the bottom of the trapdoor with its fangs.

trilobite (*157*)
Length: 1 to 4 inches (2½ to 10 centimeters)
Habitat: warm, shallow seas and sea floors
Diet: plankton, algae, and other marine animals
Fact: Trilobites flourished from 520 million years ago to 250 million years ago, making their 17,000 species one of the most successful animal groups in the history of the earth.

trumpetfish (*75*)
Length: 24 inches (61 centimeters)
Habitat: coral reefs worldwide
Diet: fish and shrimp
Fact: The trumpetfish changes color to help it blend in with its surroundings and sneak up on its prey.

tubeworm (giant tubeworm) (*140*)
Length: 8 feet (2½ meters)
Habitat: near volcanic hydrothermal vents on the floor of the Pacific Ocean
Diet: sulfur-loving bacteria
Fact: These worms are part of an unusual ecological community — one of

the few that do not depend on energy from the sun.

turkey vulture (*12, 148*)
Wingspan: 6 feet
(1¾ meters)
Habitat: southern Canada through southern South America
Diet: carrion
Fact: By riding thermals — rising currents of warm air — turkey vultures can soar for hours without flapping their wings.

Tyrannosaurus rex
(*146, 162*)
Length: 40 feet (12 meters)
Habitat: North America
(65 million years ago)
Diet: other dinosaurs, reptiles, and mammals; perhaps carrion
Fact: Its huge head, jaws, and teeth suggest that a *T. rex* could tear off a 500-pound (227-kilogram) chunk of meat in one bite.

vampire bat (*64*)
Wingspan: 7 inches
(18 centimeters)
Habitat: Central and South America
Diet: mammal blood
Fact: If the bat's victim is furry or hairy, the bat uses its teeth as a razor and shaves a patch of skin before feeding.

viceroy butterfly (*92*)
Wingspan: 3 inches
(7½ centimeters)
Habitat: meadows and marshes throughout North America
Diet: flower nectar and the juices of dead animals
Fact: Except for a black line that runs across its lower wings, this insect looks almost exactly like a monarch butterfly,

walrus (*59*)
Length: up to 11½ feet
(3½ meters)
Weight: up to 3,700 pounds
(1,678 kilograms)
Habitat: sea ice and coastlands near the Arctic Circle
Diet: clams, mussels, fish, and soft-bodied sea floor animals
Fact: The walrus's tusks can reach three feet (91 centimeters) in length. It uses them to haul itself out of the water and to break breathing holes in the sea ice from below.

warthog (*105*)
Weight: 250 pounds
(113 kilograms)
Habitat: central and southern Africa
Diet: grass, leaves, roots, and tubers

Fact: Warthogs live in groups called sounders.

water bear (*143*)
Length: ¹⁄₁₀₀ inch
(¼ millimeter)
Habitat: worldwide in almost every environment, including polar ice caps, hot springs, deserts, rainforests, and the deep ocean
Diet: plants and bacteria
Fact: Water bears were launched into orbit on a satellite without protection against the cold and vacuum of space. When they returned to earth 10 days later, most of the little creatures were still alive.

weeverfish (*94*)
Length: 6 inches
(15 centimeters)
Habitat: the eastern Atlantic Ocean and the Mediterranean Sea
Diet: shrimp and small fish
Fact: Unlike most fish, the weeverfish does not have a swim bladder — an air-filled organ that keeps it buoyant. If it stops swimming, it will sink to the bottom.

white tern (*33*)
Length: 10 inches
(25 centimeters)
Habitat: small tropical islands
Diet: small fish
Fact: The white tern lives on islands where there are no predators. Otherwise, its practice of laying an egg on a bare tree branch would probably never have evolved.

wild turkey (*27*)
Weight: 20 pounds
(9 kilograms)
Habitat: throughout much of North America
Diet: grass, nuts, seeds, fruit, and small animals
Fact: Unlike the domestic turkey, the wild turkey is a fast and agile flyer, attaining speeds of 50 miles per hour (80 kilometers per hour).

wild water buffalo (*137*)
Weight: 2,600 pounds
(1,179 kilograms)
Habitat: India and Southeast Asia
Diet: grass and aquatic plants
Fact: There are only a few thousand of these buffalo left, and because their habitat is being destroyed by human activity, it's likely that they will soon become extinct in the wild.

wood frog (*142*)
Length: 2 inches
(5 centimeters)
Habitat: northern United States and Canada
Diet: insects and other invertebrates
Fact: The wood frog can survive being frozen because it has a special chemical in its blood that acts as a kind of antifreeze.

yellow tang (*104*)
Length: 8 inches
(20 centimeters)
Habitat: coral reefs in the Pacific and Indian Oceans
Diet: algae and plants
Fact: Tang are popular aquarium fish, but to avoid a serious cut, people must handle them very carefully.

acidic
Having the qualities of or containing acid, a sour-tasting chemical substance that in strong concentrations reacts destructively with metal and organic material.

appendage
A part of the body that extends or projects, such as an antenna or a leg.

aquatic
Living in or taking place in water, either salt or fresh.

Arctic Circle
An imaginary line circling the earth about 1,600 miles (2,600 kilometers) south of the North Pole. North of this line, the sun does not set at the summer solstice (the longest day of the year) and does not rise above the horizon at the winter solstice (the shortest day).

arthropod
A large group of animals including insects, spiders, crustaceans, and centipedes. Arthropods are invertebrates. They have external skeletons and jointed limbs.

asexual reproduction
Producing offspring without a male and female parent.

bacteria
A large group of microscopic single-celled organisms found in virtually every environment on earth. Some bacteria cause disease, but many others are helpful or essential to life on earth.

biologist
A scientist who studies life and living organisms.

bioluminescence
Light produced chemically by a living organism. Most bioluminescent organisms live in the sea, but some insects and land plants also generate light.

brackish
Slightly salty water. Usually fresh water that has mixed with salt water.

budding
A form of asexual reproduction in which an extension or projection from an animal's body forms, then breaks off and becomes a new individual.

camouflage
For an animal, a disguise or method of concealment that involves looking like its surroundings.

cannibalism
An animal eating another animal of the same species.

carcass
The body of a dead animal.

carnivore
An animal — or plant — that eats other animals.

carrion
The flesh, skin, and bones of a dead animal. A source of food to scavengers.

clutch
A group of eggs laid or incubated at the same time.

coral polyp
A small, soft-bodied marine animal that lives in groups called colonies. Coral polyps produce hard skeletons that form coral reefs.

crustacean
A group of mostly aquatic animals that have jointed limbs and a hard external skeleton, including crabs, lobsters, crayfish, and shrimp. Crustaceans are a subgroup of the arthropods.

debris
Scattered pieces or parts of something that has fallen apart or been broken.

deep sea
In some definitions, the deep sea begins at 1,000 meters (3,281 feet) below the surface. No sunlight can penetrate to this depth.

disgorge
To discharge or eject forcefully, often from the mouth or stomach.

echolocation
The use of sound to navigate or search for prey. Bats, dolphins, whales, and a few other mammals—as well as some birds—echolocate by producing a series of squeaks or clicks and listening for the echoes.

environment
Everything — including light, air, water, soil, and other organisms — that surrounds and affects an animal.

evolution
The gradual change in organisms from generation to generation, often resulting in the appearance of new species.

exoskeleton
A jointed, hard outer covering or shell that supports and protects the bodies of many invertebrate animals.

extinct
Describes a species that lived at one time but that has no living members; a group of organisms that has died out.

facet
One of the individual lenses of a compound eye.

fungi
A major group of organisms — a kingdom — that includes yeast, mold, and mushrooms.

Galápagos Islands
A group of volcanic islands in the Pacific Ocean about 600 miles (965 kilometers) west of Ecuador. The islands are isolated and home to many animals that are found nowhere else.

generation
All of the offspring of a parent or parents that are at the same stage of development. Also, the average time between the birth of the parents and the birth of their offspring.

gills
Organs found in many aquatic animals that extract oxygen from the water. Gills allow an animal to breathe when it is underwater.

habitat
The normal environment of an organism.

herbivore
An animal that eats only plants and plant products.

hibernate
To spend the winter sleeping or resting in a dormant state. Hibernating animals can slow down the normal activity of their bodies so that they require little or no food.

hydrothermal vent
An opening or fissure in the earth through which volcanically heated water and steam escape. On land, these vents will appear as geysers or hot springs. On the ocean floor, the dissolved minerals escaping from a vent support entire communities of organisms.

incubate
To keep eggs warm, often by sitting on them, so they will hatch.

Indo-Pacific
The warm waters of the central and western Pacific Ocean and the Indian Ocean.

invertebrates
Animals without backbones.

keratin
Fibrous tissue found in the outer layer of human skin, as well as the main component of hair and fingernails. In animals, keratin may form claws, beaks, scales, and horns.

krill
Shrimplike marine animals found in all of the world's oceans. They are an important source of food for many larger marine animals. There are more krill, by

weight, than any other animal on earth.

lagoon
A shallow body of water separated from a larger body by sand bars, coral reefs, or some other structure. Lagoons are usually thought of as marine (saltwater) features.

larva
The juvenile form of an animal that undergoes metamorphosis and changes its appearance to become an adult.

lethal
Deadly; causing death.

luminous
Lighting up; glowing.

mandibles
Mouthparts in insects and other arthropods. They are used to bite or chew food.

menagerie
A collection of wild animals for exhibition.

microorganisms
Living things that are too small to see without magnification.

microscopic
Very small; literally, too small to see without a microscope.

mimic
In the animal world, to imitate the appearance or behavior of another creature or part of the environment.

mollusk
A large group of invertebrate animals with soft bodies and, in many cases, protective shells. Includes clams, snails, squid, and octopuses. There are about 85,000 known species of mollusk.

molt
To shed old feathers, skin, or exoskeleton. A new covering will replace what is lost. Animals often molt as they grow larger.

noxious
Something that is poisonous or otherwise harmful.

offspring
The children of animal parents.

omnivore
Animals that eat both plant and animal foods.

orb
An eye or eyeball.

organic
Related to or derived from living organisms.

ovipositor
An organ used for laying eggs. It is possessed by many female insects.

parasite
An organism that gets its nutrition by living in or on the body of another organism.

pheromone
A chemical released by an animal that influences the behavior of other members of the same species.

photosynthesis
A process by which plants, algae, and some bacteria convert the energy of sunlight into chemical energy — food.

plague
A widespread, easily transmitted, and deadly disease; the bubonic plague, or Black Death, which devastated Europe and Asia in the mid-fourteenth century.

plankton
Organisms including plants, algae, bacteria, and animals that live in fresh or salt water and drift with the currents. Many are microscopic, but some, such as jellyfish, are much larger.

pollination
The transfer of pollen, an important step in the reproduction of plants. Most plants are pollinated by insects, such as bees, and other animals.

prawn
A shrimp or large shrimplike crustacean.

predator
An animal that kills and eats other animals.

prehensile
Adapted for grasping or holding something, often used in reference to the tail of an animal that can hold on to a tree branch.

primate
A group of mammals that includes monkeys, apes, humans, and lemurs.

protozoan
A major group, or kingdom, of microscopic, mostly single-celled organisms.

quadruplets
Four offspring born to one mother at the same time.

quill
The large wing or tail feather of a bird; the hollow spine of a porcupine, hedgehog, or tenrec.

regenerate
To regrow an injured or missing part of the body.

regurgitate
To vomit, or, as many birds do to feed their young, to bring undigested food back to the mouth.

reproduce
To produce offspring.

reptilian
Reptile-like in appearance or behavior.

sibling
A brother or sister.

sonar
See *echolocation*.

species
One of the basic units biologists use to organize living things. Members of the same species can breed and produce offspring.

subtropical
Parts of the world located between temperate and tropical regions.

symbiosis
The long-term interaction of two or more different organisms. Symbiosis can be helpful to both organisms, helpful to one and harmful to the other, or it can be beneficial to one organism and leave the other unaffected.

tadpole
The larval stage of a frog or toad.

temperate
Regions of the world where the climate is neither very hot nor very cold.

toxic
Poisonous.

toxin
A poison created by a living organism.

troop
A term for a group of certain animals, including monkeys, apes, and kangaroos.

venom
Animal toxin that is injected by a bite, barb, or sting.

vertebrates
Animals with backbones.

West Indies
A group of islands between the Atlantic Ocean and the Caribbean Sea. They stretch from Florida to the coast of South America.

zooplankton
Animal and protozoan plankton, a varied group of aquatic organisms that drift with the water currents.

Making Books

In many ways, making a nonfiction picture book is a long, complicated process. It involves dozens of people: an author and illustrator, of course, but also editors, art directors, researchers, copyeditors, photographers, production supervisors, printers, salespeople, and more. It is typically at least two years from the time a concept takes shape until the delivery of a printed book.

Every book starts with an idea. And ideas come from all over: a question asked by a child; a conversation with a teacher, a scientist, or a coauthor; or something read in a magazine, noticed in the backyard, or seen at a museum. An idea appears, sticks in one's mind, and gradually takes on the shape of 32 or 40 or 48 pages — or more — of words and images.

Every author has a different way of working. And even for the same author, the bookmaking process may vary from book to book. The next few pages show the typical process I go through as I work on a book.

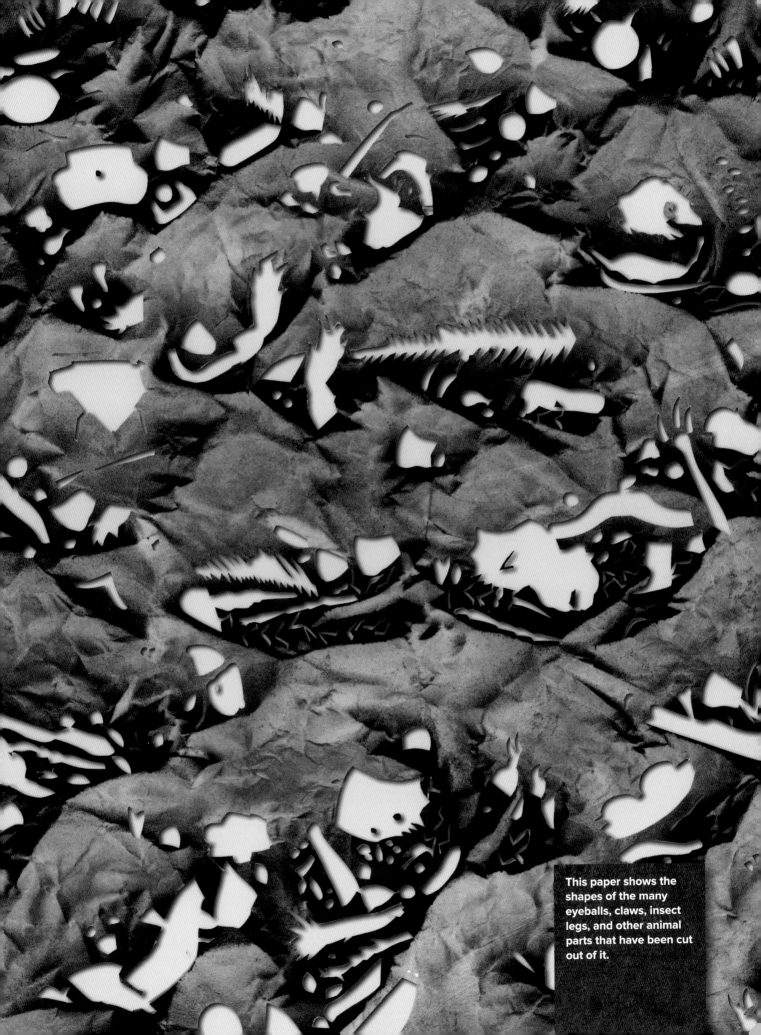

This paper shows the shapes of the many eyeballs, claws, insect legs, and other animal parts that have been cut out of it.

Where do ideas for books come from?

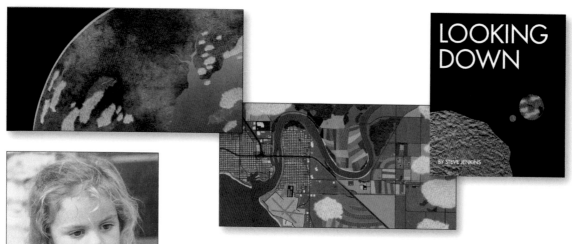

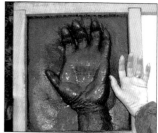

When my daughter was two or three, she looked out an airplane window and asked why the cars and houses were so small. I realized she didn't understand what she was seeing from that height. This inspired *Looking Down,* a wordless book that takes the viewer from outer space to a child's front yard.

When he was little, my older son constantly asked about animals — their size, their speed, their fierceness. His questions led to *Biggest, Strongest, Fastest,* a book of animal extremes.

On a trip to the San Diego Zoo, I saw this metal cast of a gorilla's hand. Almost every passerby held up their own hand to compare. This was the origin of *Actual Size,* a book in which all the animals — or parts of animals — are shown life-size.

Our youngest son's interest in animals and puzzles gave Robin Page and me the idea of making *I See a Kookaburra!,* a book showing creatures hidden — then revealed — in a series of different habitats.

A conversation with Robin, my wife and frequent collaborator, about animal cooperation — and our own cooperation — resulted in *How to Clean a Hippopotamus,* a book about animal symbiosis.

Watching my own dog and cat at work and play led to *Dogs and Cats,* a two-sided book about the natural history of these predators with whom we share our homes.

Research

This is a critical part of every book project. Often, as I began to explore an idea, the research itself takes me in a different direction. When researching a book concept, I become immersed in many different sources of information. It's always a little overwhelming. But if the original idea is a good one, some order gradually starts to emerge from all the facts and images.

Newspapers, magazines, nature DVDs (especially those produced by the BBC), and, of course, the Internet are all helpful.

We have a large collection of natural history books at home.

I find that libraries and bookstores are great places to research a subject or just wander around. Many times something unexpected will catch my eye.

There is a lot of inaccurate information on the Web, so facts found there need to come from a credible source or be very thoroughly checked — preferably both. Two trustworthy websites with lots of good information: Archive.org. and National Geographic.com.

I use a lot of my own photos
for reference. Some are
taken in natural settings . . .

. . . others, in zoos,
aquariums, and museums.

Sketches, thumbnails, and dummies

Once an idea for a book takes shape, the next step is to make lots of notes and little sketches, called thumbnails, exploring what might be on each page. These sketches are quick and easy to make, so it's possible to try out a lot of different ideas and not feel bad about throwing most of them out.

Move! is a book I made with Robin. It's about animals that run, dive, crawl, fly, waddle, and so on. These two pages show a few of the steps we went through as we worked on the book.

While we are working on the thumbnail layouts, I'm writing a rough draft of the book's text. I write first in a notebook, then on a computer.

We do lots of thumbnail sketches and make lists of possible animals to include.

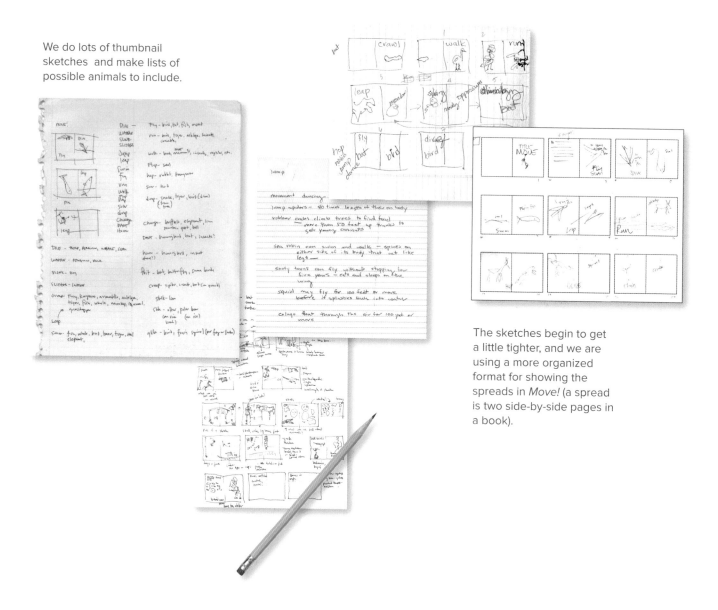

The sketches begin to get a little tighter, and we are using a more organized format for showing the spreads in *Move!* (a spread is two side-by-side pages in a book).

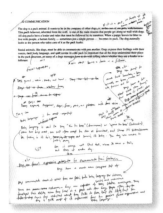

The text gets printed out, and I continue to make changes and add notes by hand.

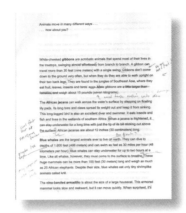

After being rewritten 10 or 12 times — a typical number of rewrites — the text is finally in manuscript form. My editor has made comments on this copy, pointing out things that are not clear or that could be said in a better way.

Robin does more precise sketches of the animals and combines them with headlines.

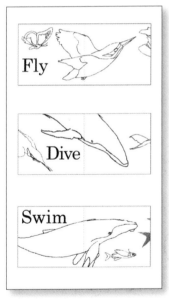

These sketches are created on a graphics tablet attached to a computer. It's like tracing a photo on the computer screen.

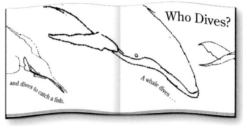

When the sketch layouts are finished, they are trimmed, folded, and stapled into a dummy — a rough version of the book. This helps us see how the sequence of words and images is working.

The first dummy is black and white. Text from the manuscript has been combined with sketches of the animals.

As a book is coming to life, a lot of things are going on at the same time. The black and white dummy has given me a good idea of how the book will look, so I start creating the final illustrations while design and text options are still being explored (the illustration process is described on the next page).

We make color prints that include copies of the finished illustrations and the final text. When these prints are assembled into a dummy, they will give us a good idea of what the printed book will look like.

Illustration

The illustrations in my books are all cut- or torn-paper collages. Most of the papers are handmade, and many of them come from countries with a long tradition of papermaking: Japan, India, Thailand, Nepal, Mexico, France, or Italy.

3 Now I choose the paper that I'll use to make the whale. There is often an element of surprise here, as I usually don't know what paper I'll end up working with.

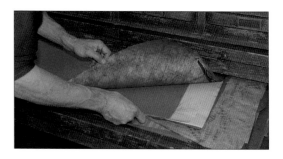

Most of my papers are stored in a large flat file, organized by color.

1 Finding references is the first step. I collect several different photos and illustrations of the animal I'm going to work with.

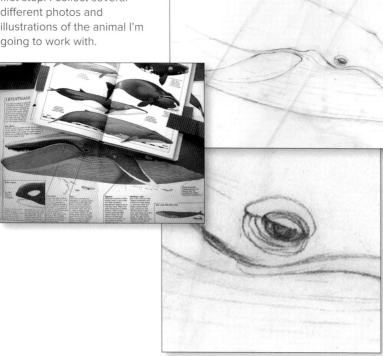

2 Using the reference images and sketch layouts as a guide, I make a series of pencil drawings. I work on tracing paper so I can trace and refine my own sketches. I don't trace the original reference — that seems to take some of the life out of the illustration. The imperfections that are part of my sketching process seem to give an animal more personality.

I will use photocopies of the sketch as templates when I cut shapes out of color paper, so I draw the lines exactly where I want the paper to be cut.

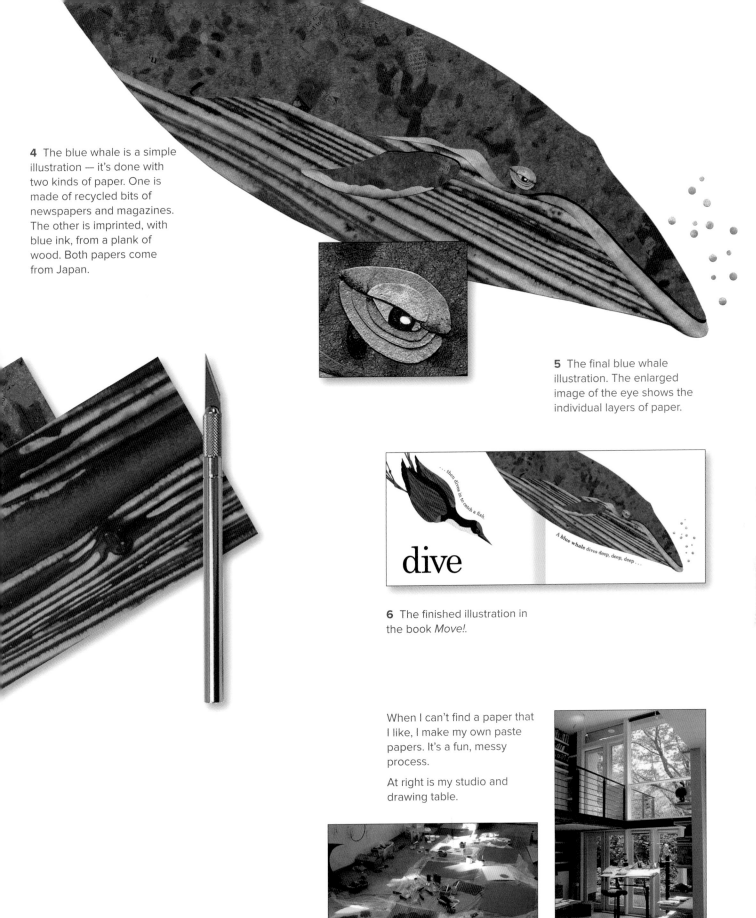

4 The blue whale is a simple illustration — it's done with two kinds of paper. One is made of recycled bits of newspapers and magazines. The other is imprinted, with blue ink, from a plank of wood. Both papers come from Japan.

5 The final blue whale illustration. The enlarged image of the eye shows the individual layers of paper.

6 The finished illustration in the book *Move!*.

dive

. . . then dives in to catch a fish.

A blue whale dives deep, deep, deep . . .

When I can't find a paper that I like, I make my own paste papers. It's a fun, messy process.

At right is my studio and drawing table.

Making a book – a timeline

How long does it take to make a book? It varies —
some books involve more research; others have more
complex illustrations that take longer to create. But
every book goes through the same basic process.

This is a timeline for *The Beetle Book*.

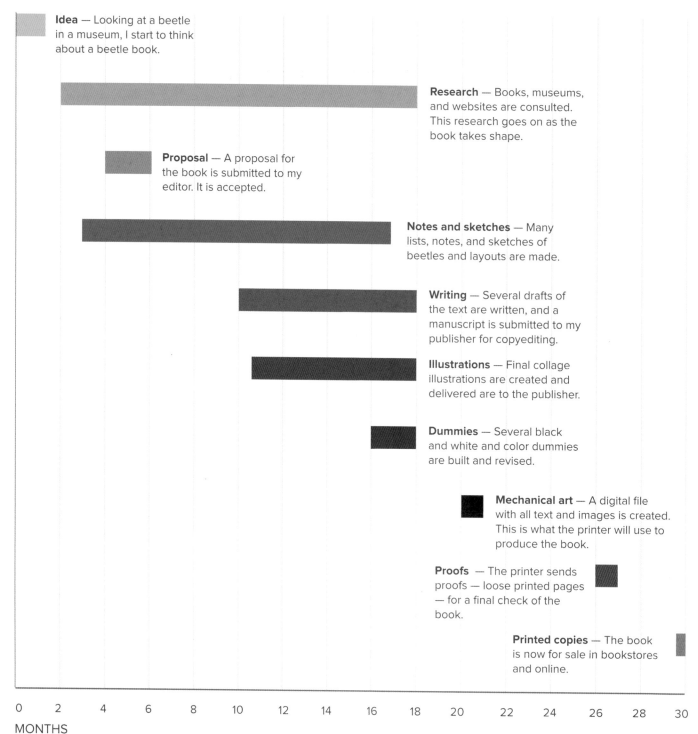

Idea — Looking at a beetle
in a museum, I start to think
about a beetle book.

Research — Books, museums,
and websites are consulted.
This research goes on as the
book takes shape.

Proposal — A proposal for
the book is submitted to my
editor. It is accepted.

Notes and sketches — Many
lists, notes, and sketches of
beetles and layouts are made.

Writing — Several drafts of
the text are written, and a
manuscript is submitted to my
publisher for copyediting.

Illustrations — Final collage
illustrations are created and
delivered are to the publisher.

Dummies — Several black
and white and color dummies
are built and revised.

Mechanical art — A digital file
with all text and images is created.
This is what the printer will use to
produce the book.

Proofs — The printer sends
proofs — loose printed pages
— for a final check of the
book.

Printed copies — The book
is now for sale in bookstores
and online.

0   2   4   6   8   10   12   14   16   18   20   22   24   26   28   30

MONTHS

A stag beetle from
The Beetle Book

Adventures Among Ants.
By Mark W. Moffet. University of California Press, 2010.

Alligators and Crocodiles
By Malcolm Penny. Crescent Books, 1991.

Amazing Animal Facts.
Edited by Joe Elliot and Jayne Miller. Dorling Kindersley, 2003.

Amazing Biofacts.
By Susan Goodman. Peter Bedrick Books, 1983.

Amazing Numbers in Biology.
By Rainer Flindt. Springer, 1996.

Animal Fact File.
By Dr. Tony Hare. Checkmark Books, 1999.

Animal Life.
By Charlotte Uhlenbroek. Dorling Kindersley, 2008.

Animal Life.
By Heidi & Hans-Jürgen Koch. H.F. Ullmann. Tandem Verlag GmbH, 2008.

Animal Life: Form and Function in the Animal Kingdom.
By Jill Bailey. Oxford University Press, 1994.

Animal Records.
By Mark Carwardine. Sterling, 2008.

Animal Senses.
By Pamela Hickman. Kids Can Press, 1998.

Another World: Colors, Textures, and Patterns of the Deep.
By Dos Winkel. Prestel, 2005.

The Book of Comparisons.
By The Diagram Group. Sidgwick & Jackson, 1980.

Children's Encyclopedia of the Animal Kingdom.
Edited by Dr. Graham Bateman. Dorset Press, 1992.

Coral Reefs.
By Les Holliday. Tetra Press, 1989.

Creatures of the Deep.
Erich Hoyt. Firefly Books, 2001.

Dangerous Animals.
Edited by Dr. John Seidensticker and Dr. Susan Lumpkin. The Nature Company Discoveries Library, 1995.

Dazzled and Deceived: Mimicry and Camouflage.
Peter Forbes. Yale University Press, 2009.

The Deep.
By Claire Nouvian. University of Chicago Press, 2007.

Dramatic Displays.
By Tim Knight. Heinemann Library, 2003.

The Egg.
By Gallimard Jeunesse and Pascale de Bourgoing. Scholastic, 1989.

Eggs: Nature's Perfect Package.
By Robert Burton. Facts on File Publications, 1987.

The Encyclopedia of Animals.
Edited by Dr. Per Christiansen. Amber Books, 2006.

Encyclopedia of Mammals.
Edited by Dr. Edwin Gould and Dr. George McKay. Academic Press, 1990.

Exploding Ants.
By Joann Settel. Atheneum Books for Young Readers, 2000.

Extraordinary Animals.
By Ross Piper. Greenwood Press, 2007.

Extreme Nature.
By Mark Carwardine. HarperCollins, 2005.

The Golden Treasury of Natural History.
By Bertha Morris Parker. Simon and Schuster, 1952.

Life in the Undergrowth.
By David Attenborough. Princeton University Press, 2005.

Life of Mammals.
By David Attenborough. Princeton University Press, 1999.

Living in the Wild.
Consultant: Michael Chinery. Southwater, 2002.

Marine Life of the Pacific and Indian Oceans.
By Gerald Allen. Periplus, 2000.

Nature's Champions: The Biggest, the Fastest, the Best.
By Alvin and Virginia Silverstein. Random House, 1980.

Nature's Predators.
By Michael Bright, Robin Kerrod, and Barbara Taylor. Hermes House, 2000.

Nature's Ways.
By Roy Chapman Andrews. Avenel Books, 1951.

On Size and Life.
By Thomas A. McMahon and John Tyler Bonner. Scientific American Library, 1983.

The Private Lives of Animals.
Edited by Milton Rugoff and Ann Guilfoyle. Grosset & Dunlap, 1974.

Reptiles and Insects.
Edited by Dr. Glenn Shea and Dan Bickel. Fog City Press, 2003.

Secret Worlds.
By Stephen Dalton. Firefly Books, 1999.

The Sibley Guide to Birds.
By David Allen Sibley. Alfred A. Knopf, 2000.

The Smaller Majority.
By Piotr Naskrecki. Harvard University Press, 2005.

The Usborne Book of Animal Facts.
Anita Ganeri. Usborne Publishing, 1988.

Venom, Poison, and Electricity.
By Kimberley Jane Pryor. Marshall Cavendish, 2010.

The Way Nature Works.
Edited by Jill Bailey. MacMillan Publishing Company, 1997.

Wildlife Factfinder.
Martin Walters. Dempsey Parr, 1999.

Some of the illustrations and information in this book have appeared in other books I've written or co-written, including the following titles:

Actual Size.
Houghton Mifflin Harcourt, 2004.

Almost Gone: The World's Rarest Animals.
HarperCollins, 2006.

Animals in Flight.
Written with Robin Page.
Houghton Mifflin Harcourt, 2010.

The Beetle Book.
Houghton Mifflin Harcourt, 2012.

Big and Little.
Houghton Mifflin Harcourt, 1996.

Biggest, Strongest, Fastest.
Houghton Mifflin Harcourt, 1995.

Bones.
Scholastic, 2010.

Dogs and Cats.
Houghton Mifflin Harcourt, 2007.

Down, Down, Down.
Houghton Mifflin Harcourt, 2008.

How Many Ways Can You Catch a Fly?
Written with Robin Page.
Houghton Mifflin Harcourt, 2008.

How to Clean a Hippopotamus.
Written with Robin Page.
Houghton Mifflin Harcourt, 2010.

I See a Kookaburra!
Written with Robin Page.
Houghton Mifflin Harcourt, 2005.

Just a Second.
Houghton Mifflin Harcourt, 2011.

Life on Earth: The Story of Evolution.
Houghton Mifflin Harcourt, 2002.

Living Color.
Houghton Mifflin Harcourt, 2007.

Move!
Written with Robin Page.
Houghton Mifflin Harcourt, 2006.

My First Day.
Written with Robin Page.
Houghton Mifflin Harcourt, 2013.

Never Smile at a Monkey.
Houghton Mifflin Harcourt, 2009.

Prehistoric Actual Size.
Houghton Mifflin Harcourt, 2005.

Sisters and Brothers.
Written with Robin Page.
Houghton Mifflin Harcourt, 2008.

Slap, Squeak, and Scatter.
Houghton Mifflin Harcourt, 2001.

Time for a Bath.
Written with Robin Page.
Houghton Mifflin Harcourt, 2011.

Time to Eat.
Written with Robin Page.
Houghton Mifflin Harcourt, 2011.

Time to Sleep.
Written with Robin Page.
Houghton Mifflin Harcourt, 2011.

What Do You Do When Something Wants to Eat You?
Houghton Mifflin Harcourt, 2001.

What Do You Do with a Tail Like This?
Written with Robin Page.
Houghton Mifflin Harcourt, 2003.

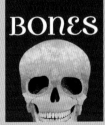

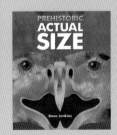

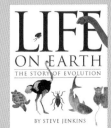

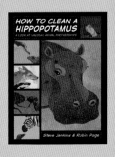

For Robin

www.hmhco.com

The text of this book is set in ITC Garamond
The illustrations are torn- and cut-paper collage.

Library of Congress Cataloging-in-Publication Data is on file.

ISBN 978-0-547-55799-1

Manufactured in China

SCP 10 9 8 7 6 5 4 3

4500507635

Thanks to the following for their kind permission to reproduce Steve Jenkins' illustrations:

skeleton, page 14.
From BONES by Steve Jenkins. Scholastic Inc./Scholastic Press.
Copyright© 2010 by Steve Jenkins. Used by permission.

vulture, page 12.
From VULTURE VIEW © 2007 by April Pulley Sayre.
Illustrations © 2007 by Steve Jenkins. Reprinted by permission of Henry Holt and Company, LLC. All rights reserved.

wren, page 9; mole, pages 9, 59; porcupine, pages 10, 96; snail, page 12; owl, page 56; smelt, page 58. From ANIMAL POEMS © 2007 by Valerie Worth. Illustrations © 2007 by Steve Jenkins. Reprinted by permission of Farrar, Straus and Giroux, LLC. All rights reserved.

Darwin's frog, page 40.
From THE MYSTERY OF DARWIN'S FROG © 2013 by Marty Crump, Ph.D. Illustrations © 2013 by Steve Jenkins. Reprinted by permission of Boyd's Mill Press.

rat, page 61; fly, page 60.
From PUG© 2013 by Valerie Worth. Illustrations © 2013 by Steve Jenkins. Reprinted by permission of Farrar, Straus and Giroux, LLC. All rights reserved.